THE FAMOUS 'BOOT' ROOM — where team plans and tactics are hatched.

ON THE MAP— Liverpool's path of conquest round Europe.

CAPTURED ON CANVAS — (above) — The European Cup; The First Division Championship Trophy; and The Milk Cup (now the Littlewoods Cup) — all won in season 1983-84.

(below) — The 1979-1980 Championship winning team.

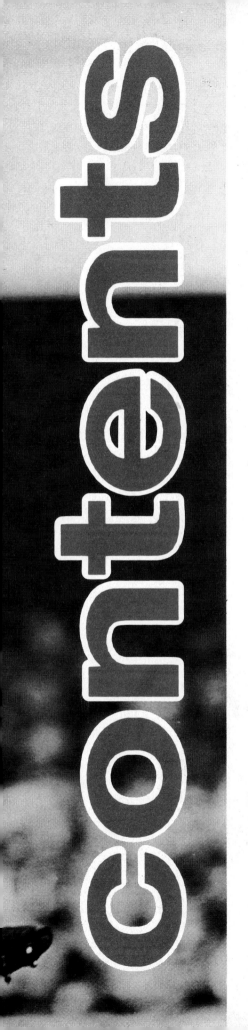

THE TOPICAL TIMES FOOTBALL BOOK

BRYAN ROBSON
Manchester United

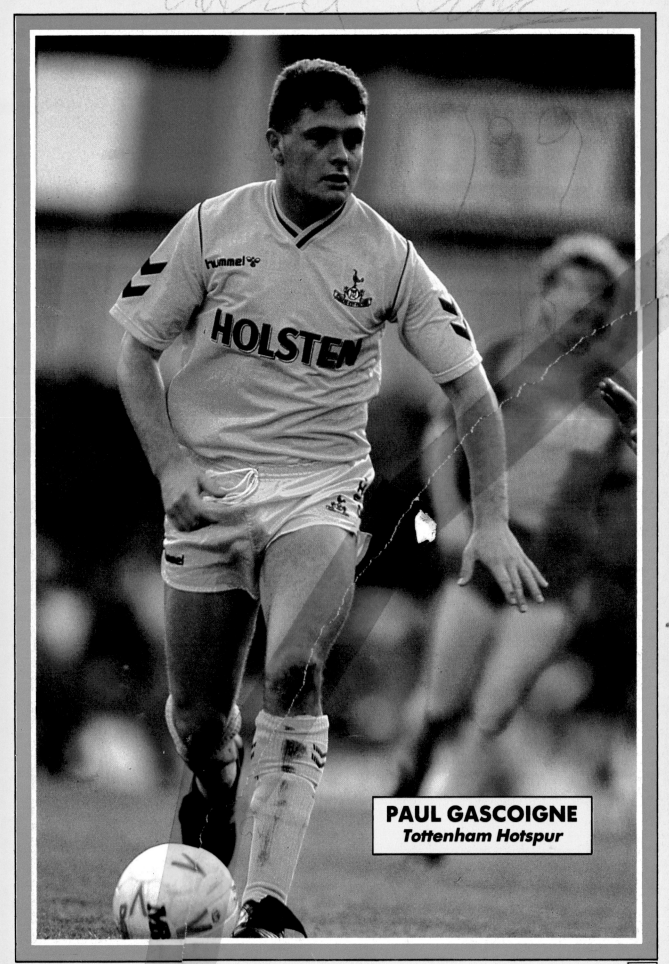

PAUL GASCOIGNE
Tottenham Hotspur

THE BEST IS YET

Arsenal's ALAN SMITH is confident about the future.

I'll always remember last season! Twenty-three League goals, a place in the England squad and a part in Arsenal's championship triumph, made it a memorable campaign. And yet I think my best is still to come.

I really wouldn't expect to be showing my true potential for another couple of years yet. I have to admit that it took me a little while to settle when I first came to Arsenal, and I didn't score as many goals as I wanted. But then again, goals are not everything in my game.

In fact I've never really considered myself to be an out- and-out goalscorer like John Aldridge, Tony Cottee or my old Leicester striking-partner, Gary Lineker. I'm quite happy if I can get 20 goals in a season.

Things really started to come good for me last season after a first year that had been a bit up and down. Throughout that tricky period I was lucky enough to have a great manager like George Graham backing me up. He was full of encouragement, letting me know that he had confidence in me and that the goals would come.

I like to think that my performances last season paid him back for his faith in me. The goals certainly helped to get some of the doubters off my back.

I was also grateful to the boss for putting the right sort of team together last term. For starters the team had much more width to it in the shape of Brian Marwood and David Rocastle.

With the sort of service those two were producing, I couldn't really fail to score goals. But I've got the whole team to thank. Everybody had a good season last year, which is the main reason we lifted the championship.

We've a lot of young players in our team — and the experience of last season will help them be even better players in the future.

My team-mates certainly played a big part in helping me to get a place in the England squad for World Cup qualifying games.

TO COME!

But a place in the squad was no guarantee of a place in the side with so much competition for places. Gary Lineker, Peter Beardsley, Nigel Clough, and Tony Cottee were just a few of the top players I had to battle it out with.

It was very good to at least train with Gary Lineker again because we had been partners at Leicester City a few years ago. I think we could do a good job together but I can't afford to be fussy about who I play with for England.

In football terms it's a long time since Gary and I were playing together regularly at club level. And there's a world of difference between that and teaming up in training a few days before an international.

We've both changed as players since we were at Leicester. Different clubs make new demands and we've had to adapt accordingly, Gary with Everton and Barcelona and myself with Arsenal.

OPPORTUNITY

Before I joined Leicester I was playing for Alvechurch in the Southern League, while studying for a degree at the same time. I was doing a course in languages at Coventry Polytechnic.

During my first year at college I scored about 25 goals for Alvechurch and those goals brought about the end of my college career. But they meant the start of my life in football because Leicester asked me to sign professional forms for them. It was too good an opportunity to miss.

My first season at Filbert Street really couldn't have gone much better. I managed to get straight in the team alongside Gary Lineker and it wasn't long before the goals started coming for both of us.

By the end of the season I'd scored 13 League goals, which, although only half the number Gary scored, pleased me. Far more important than that was the fact we were promoted from Division Two.

That gave me the chance to play in the First Division and test myself out against top defenders. One of the highlights for me that year was scoring in our 2-2 draw against Liverpool at Anfield.

In fact, in all the time that I was at Leicester we were quite a bogey team for Liverpool, even though were were usually at opposite ends of the table.

As a rule at Leicester it was a constant battle against relegation. And when I finally moved on from Filbert Street the team was on its way back down to the Second Division.

I'd been allowed to stay on at Leicester on loan after I'd signed for Arsenal. That was a last ditch attempt to keep my old club in the top flight. Only when it was a lost cause did I move on permanently. I even played against Arsenal during that period but couldn't stop my new club beating us 4-1.

Despite that I left Leicester with some good memories as well as one very painful one. Back in my first season in Division One I'd played against Stoke City. One of their defenders that day was Steve Bould and at one point in the match he accidentally caught me in the mouth with his boot.

Three of my teeth went flying! But thankfully the physio picked them up, packed them in ice and took me off to hospital. An emergency operation was successful and the teeth were replaced with the aid of a brace.

What I didn't know then was that one day I would be playing in the same team as Steve Bould. But, of course, he joined me at Arsenal last season. I try to avoid getting in the way of his boots!

When I did finally join Arsenal I knew that my first task was to establish myself as a regular in the team. However much money George Graham might have paid for me I was still expected to do my stuff to merit my place.

At first I thought that Charlie Nicholas was going to be my striking partner.

But things didn't quite work out like that. Charlie was left out after four games and I had a number of different partners after that until Paul Merson started to establish himself.

Although it did take me a while to get going that season, there were still plenty of good things happening. We reached the final of the Littlewoods Cup, the F.A. Cup quarter-finals and at one stage were on top of the League.

Even at the end of the season when the team only had sixth place in the League to show for our efforts, I was reasonably satisfied. After all, I had scored 16 League and Cup goals in what people were calling a bad year.

I was confident that the next

STEVE BOULD

season would be better both for the team and me personally. And I was right.

I made a perfect start with a hat-trick on the opening day of the season at Wimbledon. By the end of October I was already in to double figures for League goals, quickly passing my total from the previous year.

And it wasn't just the goal count that was going well. I felt good about my all-round form as well. Eventually I got the reward I'd been hoping for — a place in the England squad.

I won my chance as a second half substitute in a friendly against Saudi Arabia. Then later I was given the opportunity to start a game in Greece alongside my old friend Gary Lineker.

International football is very different but I hope I get the chance to become used to it. With so much competition it won't be easy, but if I keep scoring goals for Arsenal I must be in with a chance.

I would love to play in the World Cup in Italy. But before that I want to help Arsenal win another Division One title. That'll prove that last season's success was not a flash in the pan.

ON SHOW

TAKE A LOOK AT GRAHAM SMITH'S AMAZING COLLECT

WHATEVER the results of England's final World Cup qualifying matches, one Englishman is guaranteed an official place at the finals in Italy.

Londoner Graham Smith has dipped into his extensive collection of football memorabilia to help the World Cup organisers put together a soccer exhibition that will tour Italy before the Finals, and go on display in Rome during the competition.

In twenty years of collecting, Graham has amassed a remarkable collection of football items; old international caps and shirts; F.A. Cup-winners medals; League Championship medals; badges and souvenirs; thousands of soccer postcards and cigarette cards; hundreds of international match programmes; and a number of different football games.

Graham provided some items for the Football Association at the time of the F.A.'s 125th Anniversary celebrations. This attracted interest from the Italians who wanted to stage a special football exhibition to mark their staging of the World Cup.

Representatives from the Italian organisers flew to London to look through Graham's collection and arranged to borrow various items to exhibit.

Graham also has some of his collection on loan at a new 'Sports Legends' permanent sports exhibition at Mevagissey, in Cornwall, and in the Austrian National Football Museum in Vienna.

A Chelsea fan as a youngster, Graham's collection began in a relatively small way with programmes and autographs.

"I built up a very good collection of England international programmes from home and away games — I must have around 300 now, and lack only one England programme since the war," says Graham.

"I decided I would like to have an England cap and shirt to go with the programmes. I managed to obtain Martin Peters'

England cap from a match against Holland. He'd donated it to a charity auction, and I acquired it from the person who bought it, in exchange for some valuable programmes.

"Once I had the cap, everything snowballed from there. I now have about 45 international caps. The oldest is Irish, dating back to 1889. I believe it is the oldest Irish international cap in existence.

"Then I began to collect everything connected with football — shirts, medals, badges, postcards, cigarette cards, games, posters, souvenirs as well as caps and programmes.

"My oldest item dates back to October 26, 1863. It is a copy of The Times containing an article about the formation of the Football Association at a meeting of captains and representatives of leading clubs."

Graham has what may be a unique collection of programmes. He has a near complete set of match programmes for each First Division Championship winning team in every season since the war.

In addition he has a vast collection of F.A. Cup Final, semi-final and big match programmes. Plus a collection of 'special interest' issues.

"Rather than just quantity I've tried to collect programmes that for some reason are of particular interest," he says. "I have aimed to obtain the programmes from each club's record attendance

A selection of international jerseys — including those of Gordon Banks, Alan Rough and Martin Peters.

match, and from other significant matches."

Graham searches for items at auctions, postcard fairs, market stalls, antique shops and the like.

One of his most interesting items is the international cap awarded to John Goodall, captain of England and the Preston 'Invincibles' — the first club side to complete the Football League Championship/F.A. Cup 'double' in 1888-89.

The cap covers England appearances against Scotland between 1888 and 1898. To go with it, Graham has an England shirt of the period, which might well have been Goodall's.

And to complete the Goodall connection, there is a leather-bound Dinner Menu

Graham with a photograph of John Goodall and his international 'cap'; and the cap itself. Also in the picture, the international shirt from the 1890's which Graham believes could be John Goodall's.

from the F.A.'s 75th Anniversary Banquet signed by Goodall and everyone at his table.

Graham's ambition is to help establish a permanent football museum, where his collection can go on public display along with other items of football memorabilia.

"I can't display all my material properly at home, and I'd be very happy if somebody created a permanent museum to house it," he says.

Cigarette cards galore!

1. "International Caps and Badges" dating back to 1924.

2. "Football Club Colours".

3. "Popular Footballers" from 1910.

Some of the material that will be on display in Italy during the 1990 World Cup — including a programme autographed by the 1966 World Cup — winning England team.

A selection of International 'Caps', covering both home and foreign sides.

Produced in 1923, these silk woven pictures show club badges and colours.

Two priceless programmes. On the left that for the 1954 World Cup Final between West Germany and Hungary. Right, one for the opening game in the 1950 World Cup Finals between Brazil and Mexico.

Badges produced by the F.A. between 1899 and 1907. They were worn by players and officials at Cup Finals and Internationals.

Some of Graham's football games — several date from the 1920's and 1930's.

WHO is Liverpool's most valuable player? That question would be sure to start a long and heated argument among Liverpool fans.

After all, there are plenty of candidates. Peter Beardsley, for instance. Would you choose the Geordie for whom the Anfield club paid nearly £2 million two years ago and who has taken over Kenny Dalglish's mantle in the Liverpool side?

Would it be John Barnes, the winger bought from Watford at the same time as Beardsley and expected by many to be a flop on Merseyside?

John exploded that theory with a season-long display of dazzling skills and walked off with both Player of the Year awards in 1988.

Is it Ian Rush, whose goals for Liverpool made him the most dangerous striker in the country?

Or John Aldridge, who more than filled Rush's scoring boots during the latter's spell with Juventus, and has continued to bang in the goals since the Welshman's return?

Maybe your choice would be Steve McMahon, the midfield tiger of whom it's said that, if he plays well, Liverpool play well.

Those five would probably be the leading contenders in most arguments. But it's unlikely there would be a strong lobby for Steve Nicol, one of the quiet men of Anfield.

During his first-team career with Liverpool, the Scottish internationalist has plugged away in the shadow of the club's more expensive stars.

Public recognition was slow to arrive. Only last season did Steve feature in the end-of-season awards, runner-up in the P.F.A. vote, then first choice of the Football Writers.

Yet in his six years as a regular first-team player at Anfield, Nicol has been the club's most versatile and most consistent performer.

During that period he has probably saved the club millions of pounds in transfer fees.

When signed for £300,000 from Ayr United eight years ago, he was seen as an eventual replacement at right-back for England internationalist Phil Neal.

But Neal wasn't ready to give up his place so quickly. In the meantime, Nicol set about winning a first-team jersey in whichever position was available.

For the next few seasons, he often operated as a midfield player, filling in whenever cover was required in either full-back berths. He was even the club's emergency central defender when injuries took their toll in that department.

Steve Nicol's presence at Anfield meant there was no need for panic buying.

Faced with the simultaneous absence through injury of Alan Hansen and Gary Gillespie, most clubs would

THE QUIET MAN

ASSESSING THE VALUE OF LIVERPOOL'S STEVE NICOL

be forced to buy another centre-half. Not Liverpool, when Steve Nicol's around.

That crisis was dealt with last season without fuss as Nicol stepped into the breach.

Wherever he is asked to play, Steve adjusts to his new role without so much as a hiccup. How does he manage it?

"There's no secret," he says. "Whenever I'm given a new job to do, I simply convince myself that I am the best man available to do it.

"There's no point in going out with the belief that you're just a stand-in. If you think you are second best, then it will show in your game.

"The biggest factor, however, is the fact that when everyone in Liverpool's first-team squad is fit, I'm still confident of getting a game at full-back.

"As long as you believe you are capable of holding down a first-team spot in your proper position, that gives you the confidence to have a go anywhere.

"This allows me to tackle whatever job I am given without worrying that I might lose my place in the side if I don't play well.

"I'm as confident as any Liverpool player can be that, if things turn out badly in another position, I can still count on being switched back to full-back."

Though now one of the first names which Liverpool manager Dalglish pencils into his team-sheet every week, Nicol had a number of setbacks before he reached that status.

Several obstacles threatened his chances of ever playing for Liverpool in the first place.

One was the interest of Glasgow Rangers when he was beginning to attract attention with his performances for Ayr.

At one point he seemed set for a move to Ibrox, after the Glasgow giants made an official enquiry.

That ended in disappointment for young Nicol, however, when Rangers' valuation fell well short of the price which Ayr had put on his head.

His success with Liverpool has more than compensated for that, though he now admits there were times during his early days at Anfield when he became disheartened.

He explains, "I had more than two years in the reserves. It was murder. If ever I had a bad game — and everybody does at some stage — I'd

think to myself, what chance do I have of ever reaching the first team?

"There were 30 professionals at Anfield in those days, and young players had to go through a long spell of Central League duty before they could step up.

"I admit I became fed up. Even when I started to travel with the senior players I was going to every match as thirteenth man. I was there only as cover, and seldom had a chance of playing.

"It meant I hardly ever had a day off, because I had to train the following day due to the fact that I hadn't been involved in the match. It was a nightmare.

"At the same time, I was playing for the Scotland Under-21 side. People kept saying to me that with any other club I would have had loads of first-team games under my belt.

"Fortunately, I never became so despondent that I wanted to leave. I always felt there was a place for me in the Liverpool first team if I kept going."

That's exactly what happened, but not before Steve had to make some important sacrifices — notably cutting down on his favourite meal of fish and chips!

Steve recalls, "When I first arrived in Liverpool, I suddenly found I had hours of leisure time.

"I had never been used to having time on my hands when I played for Ayr. Though they were part-timers, they fixed me up with a labourer's job. So when I wasn't training, I was working.

"Then I signed for Liverpool, and suddenly I had more free time. I used to sit in my digs and watch TV. It was the easiest thing in the world to nip down to the chippy and get a bag of fish and chips to eat while I was lazing in front of the box. In no time at all, I'd put on more than a stone in weight!

"The trouble is the backroom staff at Anfield don't pull you aside and warn you about things like that. The club policy has always been that, in the long run, it's much better for a player to solve a problem for himself.

"Eventually the penny dropped. I cut down drastically on my visits to the chippy and got on with the job of earning a first-team place."

In succeeding with that goal, Nicol has had to be resilient. Liverpool have always had such a strong first-team squad that the worst crime a player can

commit is to be injured! Normally it means a player has to sit on the sidelines long after regaining fitness in order to win back his position from his replacement.

And during the past few years, Steve has had more than his share of worrying problems.

Three years ago, he had a stomach complaint which required surgery. But he was back in action so soon afterwards that a special dressing-room routine had to be mapped out to avoid a recurrence of the injury.

"I was ordered to improve my warm-ups in order to minimise the chance of that happening," says Steve.

"I'd always done a bit of muscle stretching before matches, of course, but had never treated the exercises seriously.

"At that time, however, I was forced to realise the importance of it, and had to be sure of going through my routine prior to training as well as matches."

On another occasion, Steve sustained a fractured jaw and had to have his teeth wired together.

He recalls, "Normally you would be expected to have to wait six weeks before going back into action and risking another knock on the jaw. But because I'm a professional player, they allowed me to cut it to four weeks.

"During the period when my teeth were wired together, however, all my food had to be liquidised. I've always retained my passion for fish and chips. One night I felt the urge for some, so I asked my wife Eleanor to put a plateful through the liquidiser. It was the worst fish supper I've ever had!"

In assessing the real value of Steve Nicol, it's not just the number of times his name hits the headlines that should be taken into account. Much more important is the week-by-week consistency which has made Steve a vital member of one of the most successful sides in the game.

But despite his success Steve is still very aware of how much he owes to others. When being presented with the Footballer of the Year award at the Football Writers' dinner, in his acceptance speech he thanked all those at Anfield — players and backroom staff alike — who had helped him. But he also made mention of Ayr United who had given him his first chance in senior football.

A nice touch from the quiet man with the giant reputation.

BARRY HORNE
Southampton

ALAN McLEARY
Millwall

THERE WERE MANY MOMENTS TO REMEMBER IN 1988-89. HOW MANY CAN YOU RECALL?

1. Who played 24 matches in goal for Liverpool during Bruce Grobbelaar's lay-off?

2. Ian Redford and Dave Beaumont both left Dundee United for English clubs. Who did they join?

3. Scunthorpe United kicked off in a brand new, purpose-built stadium. Name, please.

4. A Dutchman was voted Scotland's Player of the Year by the P.F.A. Name and club, please.

5. The Guinness Soccer Sixes tournament was a big success, but can you remember who won it?

6. Which promoted player had to twice deputise for his injured goalkeeper?

7. Which two Everton players scored twice at Wembley but still ended up with loser's medals?

8. A Scottish club hit the headlines when they missed seven successive penalty-kicks. Which team was it?

9. The first Russian ever to play in the Football League joined Ipswich from Dynamo Kiev. Can you name him?

10. Plymouth Argyle used two on-loan goalkeepers, both from Arsenal. One was Alan Miller but who was the other?

11. Which former Watford and England striker joined Bournemouth for £50,000 and scored eight goals in his first five games?

12. Name the Crystal Palace striking duo who notched 44 goals between them.

13. Which Luton Town reserve team striker cost Manchester City £600,000 last March?

14. Which clubs contested the Sherpa Van Trophy final at Wembley?

15. Which Scots winger joined Manchester United from Third Division Bristol City for £170,000?

16. Who scored the Bradford City goal which dumped highly-fancied Tottenham Hotspur out of the FA Cup in the third round?

17. Sheffield Wednesday had three managers over the course of the season. Can you name them?

18. There was just one ever-present in Chelsea's Championship-winning side. Who was he?

19. Former Manchester United favourite Kevin Moran spent his season in Spain. With which club?

20. Queen's Park Rangers smashed their pay-out record when they paid Southampton £800,000 for which Northern Ireland international?

21. Which four Second Division sides contested the promotion play-offs?

ANSWERS ON PAGE 124

CONCENTRATION!

Giving their all are Nottingham Forest's NEIL WEBB (left) and RICKY HILL (Luton).

JOHN FASHANU *Wimbledon*

JIM BETT — Aberdeen

STAR F

How GEOFF TWENTYMAN helped provide the talent for trophy-winning Liverpool.

WHEN Ian Rush, as a teenage first teamer, helped Chester's coach driver carry the playing kit to the team bus he was, unknowingly, chalking up points that would earn him a future at Liverpool.

The young Welshman's helping hand at Sealand Road paved the way to an eventual £300,000 transfer to Anfield.

Unbeknown to Rush, whilst Liverpool were secretly charting his goalscoring feats for Chester, they were also running a check on his character as well.

When Liverpool's chief scout Geoff Twentyman learnt of Rush's willingness to help, it clinched the view that his club should secure his signature.

Twentyman's findings were passed quickly on to Anfield boss Bob Paisley and Liverpool wasted no time in snapping up their man.

Such detective work is part and parcel of the job for men like Geoff Twentyman. And few could argue that the former Anfield talent-spotter outstripped them all in his time at the club.

A former Anfield player, Twentyman, after spells as a manager round the country, was brought back to the club by Bill Shankly in 1967. Twentyman's brief was to head a scouting system that would bring the cream of talent to Liverpool.

The record books show that Geoff helped formulate the most enviable and successful scouting net of modern times.

In his 20 years at the club — he's now working part-time for Glasgow Rangers — the players he recommended to successive Anfield bosses helped glean an unprecedented array of trophies for the club.

During Twentyman's time, Liverpool won ten League Championships, two FA Cups, four League Cups, four European Cups, two UEFA Cups and one Super Cup. A haul of 23 trophies.

He was the man who gave the thumbs-up to the likes of Kevin Keegan, Steve Heighway, Phil Neal, Alan Hansen, Steve Nicol and Bruce Grobbelaar.

Whilst Twentyman has done his share of unearthing unknowns, he admits that his main job was to run the rule over the slightly more mature players.

"I wasn't looking for the finished article. Nor was I concentrating on very young potential at schoolboy level," Geoff points out.

"I had to keep an eye out for and check on the slightly older players, generally out of their teens, who were capable of going into Liverpool's reserves and eventually into the first team.

CONTACTS

Twentyman's team at Liverpool consisted of a small number of scouts on the Anfield pay-roll, backed up by the hundreds of contacts he'd made over the years.

His job began when his spies passed on the whisper that a player could be Liverpool material.

"You get information on players from all angles," he goes on. "Friends, schoolteachers, managers and fans. Everyone means well. But the main asset of a good scout is to keep the rubbish away. It's a question of being able to say yes or no."

So how does Twentyman go about assessing a player?

"Firstly, in most cases I like to watch a player on his home pitch. I give them the benefit of the doubt," he points out.

"If a player does well on his home patch then I believe it will be only a matter of time, if he has what it takes, before he'll produce the goods in the more

hostile atmosphere of away grounds.

"The first thing I look for in a player is if he has good basics. As soon as a player controls a ball I can tell if he's worth noting.

"If a lad can take the sting out of a ball with one foot and pass it with the other then he's one to be looked at closely.

"Being able to read the game is the essence of a good player. A player who can see things developing and can pick out situations and exploit them has a head start on most."

Twentyman's search for Anfield's stars of the future took him all over the country and to around five matches a week.

The one thing he avoided in the main was the need to operate in disguise at stadiums. Whilst many scouts try to keep their interest in players as hush-hush as possible, Geoff did his viewing from directors' boxes.

"I recall only a couple of occasions when I needed to keep my viewing a secret," the 59-year-old continues.

"Ian Rush was a case in point. A lot of big clubs were sniffing around and Liverpool didn't want anyone to know that they were keen. I used to pay at the turnstile at Chester and stand on the terraces.

"The other time was when I was pursuing Steve Heighway at Skelmersdale United. I arrived at the ground and noticed a few other scouts hanging around. It was a case of pulling the coat collar up as far as I could so they wouldn't notice me."

Sometimes a player can fall into a scout's lap without anyone pointing him in the right direction.

"I recall Bob Paisley asking me one day to keep my eye open for a right-back because he was making plans to replace Chris Lawler in the near future," says Geoff.

"I hadn't any names in the pipeline but the very next match I went to was a Northampton

INDER!

schoolboy trialists off the train at Lime Street in Liverpool and see them settled into their digs.

"Alan Hansen was one of the youngsters we rejected. We sent him back up to Scotland because he was no better than any of the kids we had at the time.

"About three years later he was a regular in Partick Thistle's first team and I went to have another look at him when I heard quite a number of clubs were fancying him.

THUMBS-UP

"This time I knew he had what it took. The only thing that bothered me was I'd never seen him face a striker running at him chasing a ball over the top.

"I wanted to see how he coped in that situation. But it never arose when I went to see him. However, I couldn't wait forever for it to happen and I gave the thumbs-up to him anyway."

The most bizarre incidents that convinced Geoff that Liverpool should sign a player came when the man in question scored a penalty and then in another match went on a brilliant solo run . . . and he was the goalkeeper!

"I hardly need explain that the player was Bruce Grobbelaar," he went on. "Bruce was on loan to Crewe from Vancouver Whitecaps and I went to have a look at him.

"He was a real entertainer and scored from the spot. I took Bob Paisley along with me next match and when Bruce started dribbling upfield he did it so well that Bob and I were hooked. The fact he'd done nothing wrong between the sticks helped as well!"

If championships had been handed out for successes in the scouting field, then Geoff Twentyman would certainly have added a few more trophies to Liverpool's cabinet during his time at Anfield.

Town game. I took an instant liking to Phil Neal.

"I watched him a couple of times very soon after that and the more I watched him the more I realised that we'd have to get in very quickly if we wanted to snap him up without any opposition.

"Within weeks of my first seeing him, Bob Paisley had signed Phil and the right-back situation was sorted out.

"Phil Neal went on to play for England and by the time he left Anfield to go into management, he'd won more medals with Liverpool than anyone in the club's history."

Whereas Phil Neal stung Twentyman into action straight away, there are those whose names remain in the pending tray for months on end. Steve Nicol's was such a name.

"The late Jock Stein tipped me off about Steve Nicol," he says. "I

went up to Perth in Scotland to see him playing for Ayr United against St Johnstone and although he was a fit lad he looked very ordinary that night.

"I watched him on and off for a season and a half at Ayr and gradually all the good things in his game started to come out.

"I saw him come away with the ball in the full-back position once and he took the ball the full length of the field in ankle-deep mud. I knew then he was becoming a bit special.

"By the time we'd signed him he was the only player whom I ever felt confident enough in to predict that he'd play for his country at full cap level."

Even when Liverpool let someone slip from their grasp it doesn't always mean they are gone forever.

Twentyman explains, "One of the jobs I had to do was meet

PHIL GEE *Derby County*

LAST season wasn't the most memorable in Newcastle United's history. The entire campaign was spent at the wrong end of the First Division table.

But, for me personally, last term must still be marked down as the best and most important of my career. The one when I finally had a long run of first-team appearances as a central defender. And not before time, at that!

In four previous years at St James's Park I'd managed the grand total of just seven big-team games.

I was approaching 22, no longer a 'babe' in the game, and knew for a fact that if I didn't make some kind of breakthrough this time, I'd need to think about going elsewhere, even if it meant dropping down a division or two.

In fact, I was beginning to wonder if what former Middlesbrough manager Willie Maddren had said to me five years earlier was about to be proved spot on.

I'd signed on at Ayresome Park under a YTS scheme when Malcolm Allison was manager. I was just 16 at the time and thought I had taken my first major step on the soccer ladder.

Twelve months later that dream was cruelly shattered when I was

again. The chance I thought had passed me by was there for the taking.

It's also fair to say that I've loved every minute of the time I've been with Newcastle since. The club may have had its share of ups and downs, but it always has and always will be a special place to play football.

What was even more important, however, was that, during the course of last term, I managed to convince not one, but two managers that I did have the ability to be considered regular first-team material.

I'd worked very hard for my chance during pre-season the summer before last. In fact, I was pretty disappointed when I could make only the subs' bench for our opening two games of the season.

But that frustration was soon forgotten when Willie McFaul, Newcastle boss at that time, gave me the nod.

When Willie departed as manager, however, my own fortunes seemed to take a dive again. Colin Suggett took over as caretaker-manager for a spell and within a couple of matches I was back in the reserves. I didn't make the starting line-up again for two months. Not until Jim Smith arrived from Q.P.R. as team boss. Because of injury to Andy Thorn, he brought me back in almost

CONFIDENCE
IS A MUST!

So says Newcastle United's KEVIN SCOTT.

shown the door along with the advice from Willie Maddren that it might be better of I considered dropping down a couple of divisions to find my level.

The idea of that was bad enough. But when no club offered me even that chance I reckoned it might be a case of me having to abandon all thoughts of becoming a full-time professional footballer!

I had trials with Darlington and Leicester, but neither club took it any further than that. I ended up back in junior football.

That's where I stayed, too, for the best part of the following year. It was then I received an out-of-the-blue call from Newcastle to come to St James' Park and take part in a couple of matches.

Next thing I was being handed a contract. I was in League football

straight away. There I remained for the rest of the campaign.

During that time Mr Smith said one or two very nice things about me . . . and backed them all up by handing me an improved two-year extension to my contract. That came as a tremendous boost to my confidence.

Funnily enough, confidence, or rather the lack of it, was probably one of the things that held me back in my early years. Many folk told me that I was just too quiet for a big lad.

Over the past 12 months or so, however, I've developed much greater self-belief.

Not, I suppose, that I'll ever be one of the game's extroverts. It's simply not my style. What I do like to believe is that my play is doing my talking for me now.

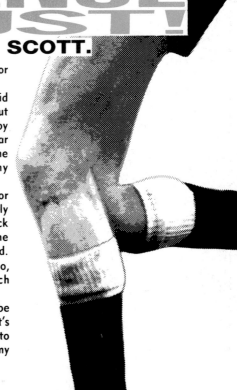

Two down, and one to go — that's the situation with my footballing ambitions at the moment. When I was a youngster in South Africa, learning everything I could about professional football in England, I had three great aims.

I wanted to play First Division football. I wanted to play in a Cup Final at Wembley. And I wanted to play international football — for somebody.

Last season I achieved my second target when I played for Luton Town in the Littlewoods Cup Final against Nottingham Forest.

I had achieved the first a year or two before, with Chelsea, and now I have set my sights on playing at international level.

I know I have a long way to go, but at least I have more than one string to my bow. I believe I could qualify to play for four different countries!

I was born in South Africa, and I travel on a South African passport. At the present time, South Africa is not a member of FIFA, so we are unable to play representative matches, but it's not impossible that we could be re-admitted in the future.

My mother is Scottish. Her maiden name was MacDonald, and I would be very proud to represent her country.

My father comes from West Germany, and so I am also qualified to play for Germany. However, I don't know the language, or the style of football, so I would probably rule them out — although I'd certainly think about it if I was asked.

And my wife is American. I played out there with Tampa Bay Rowdies for quite a few years, and I'd seriously consider lining up for the States.

With the World Cup finals being played there in 1994, it would be quite an exciting prospect to think about. Knowing how the Americans go about things, I believe their World Cup Finals will be the best ever staged.

In the States they treat sportsmen unbelievably well. Top players in any sport are celebrities much more than they are in Britain.

I enjoyed playing for Tampa Bay. I loved the life-style and the way the game was presented.

But I was on the first plane to London when I had the opportunity to join an English club. I always wanted to play club football at the highest level possible, and that meant the English First Division. As far as I'm concerned it's the most competitive league in the world, and I jumped at the chance to sign for Chelsea.

There's nothing anywhere to match the tradition and history of the English League. I couldn't wait to play my first match in the First Division for Chelsea.

However, I've got to admit that my experience at Chelsea was a little disappointing. I never felt I was given a chance to establish a place in the side. My game is all about using my skills to take players on. When Chelsea signed me they knew what my strengths were, yet I was steered away from using my skills.

I feel every player needs a manager with a bit of faith in his ability. You need a bit of encouragement to be able to produce your best. At Chelsea it seemed I was just being discouraged from playing my

An ambitious h

That's the

aim of

Luton Town's

ROY WEGERLE.

24

natural game. They were trying to change me into something that I couldn't be — a winger who had to play like a midfield player or a full-back.

I got very depressed over it. At the end of my second season at Stamford Bridge, I was at rock bottom. The club was sliding out of the First Division, and I was stuck in the reserves with no real future.

Sometimes I felt like quitting altogether, but every time it came into my mind, I thought 'I haven't come all this way to give up this early'.

In the end, Luton Town came in to sign me, and I'll always be grateful to manager Ray Harford. He

saved my career. He encouraged me to use my skills — as long as it was within the framework of the team. Ray gave me my head to take on defenders. Not many managers are prepared to let players do that in England.

In the States there were always a lot of very skilful players from the Latin countries — South Americans mostly. It was a very continental type of game, with a slow build-up, and then a rat-tat-tat of one-twos around the box.

It's much more physical in England, and I had to adjust to the different approach. At Luton I at least had a manager who believed in my ability, and was prepared to let me play.

I was labelled as a winger at Chelsea, but I never really enjoyed playing out wide. I always wanted the chance to play down the centre, and Ray Harford gave me that chance at Luton.

It could hardly have been better for me, because playing alongside

Mick Harford is a dream for a player like myself. He's so dominant in the air, wins so many challenges, that there are always chances cropping up.

Failing to establish myself at Chelsea made me all the more determined to achieve something with Luton. We so nearly did it in the Littlewoods Cup. I'm convinced we were only inches away from winning the trophy.

When we were leading 1-0, early in the second half, Forest defenders Steve Sutton and Terry Wilson got into a mix-up, and let in Mick Harford. Unfortunately Mick didn't get a proper touch, and the ball was left bouncing towards the net.

I was just a yard away from it, but Forest full-back Brian Laws got there first and cleared the situation. Had the ball crossed the line, things might have been very different.

That was the moment we needed a bit of luck — and we didn't get it. Shortly after, they got a penalty to equalise, and that was that. Forest went on to win 3-1.

It was very disappointing to lose, more so because I felt I didn't do myself justice. But it was still a great occasion for me to play at Wembley. The crowd was fantastic, and the pitch was great. I will always remember the occasion — but I hope to be back again in the future to reverse the result.

My parents flew over for the match from South Africa. They had watched me before in America, but it was the first time they'd seen me play in England. It would have made their day to have seen us win the cup, but it was not to be.

As a schoolboy in South Africa I played with Richard Gough, who is now an established Scottish international with Glasgow Rangers.

We were both recommended to English clubs by Roy Bailey, the one-time Ipswich goalkeeper and father of former Manchester United 'keeper, Gary Bailey. Richard went to Charlton for a trial, and I went up to Manchester United. Things didn't work out for either of us, and we went back to South Africa. But later, Richard got another chance with Dundee United, and signed as a professional for them.

I decided to try my luck in the United States, and was signed by Tampa Bay. When I first went there, in the early 80's, a lot of top names were there. Soccer was really big, and there were occasionally crowds of 50,000. But after a few years the game began to go downhill and that was when I began looking towards the English League.

It's great to have achieved two of my ambitions in the game. Now I'm going all out to win that first international cap — if somebody wants me.

RAY HARFORD

GRAHAM KELLY became the most powerful man in English football when he took over last season as Chief Executive of the Football Association after almost ten years as Secretary of the Football League. He became the first professional administrator to have headed the two major football authorities in England.

In his twenty years at Lytham St. Annes, headquarters of the Football League, he understudied the late Alan Hardaker, a leader of great authority and vision, before succeeding him as Secretary in 1979. Last season he took over at Lancaster Gate from the retiring Secretary, Ted Croker, in the newly-created post of Chief Executive.

Having steered the Football League through the problems of beating hooliganism; dealing with the tragedies of Bradford and Heysel (and the consequent isolation from Europe); negotiating new contracts with television; breaking new ground with regular 'live' televised matches; and reducing the First Division to 20 clubs, Mr Kelly was well qualified to lead the Football Association into the 1990's. And he wasn't long in his post when he showed his qualities when he piloted the F.A. through the controversy and problems of the Hillsborough disaster.

Another early task that Mr Kelly set himself was to catch up on the tradition and history of the F.A. Our cameras went with him round Lancaster Gate headquarters.

The trophy cabinet in the entrance hall at Lancaster Gate.

KELLY'S KINGDOM

a look behind the scenes at Football Association Headquarters with Chief Executive Graham Kelly.

In the reception room at Lancaster Gate, Graham Kelly admires some of the gifts and trophies presented to the Football Association on foreign tours or by visiting teams.

In his office, Graham examines a magnificent silver cup. It is a replica of the second F.A. Cup trophy, won by Manchester United in 1909. The real trophy was presented in 1911 to Lord Kinnaird for his services to the game. The replica at Lancaster Gate was commissioned by Manchester United, and presented to a J.H. Davis of Mosely Hall, 'in appreciation of his services to the club'.

The famous wooden balls used to make the draw for the F.A. Cup. This particular set of 32 balls, and the equally famous blue velvet bag, has been in use for about twenty years. There are about four sets of balls at Lancaster Gate, and the F.A. is currently looking for a supplier of a new set. They are made of hard wood and numbered in white paint.

The library at Lancaster Gate contains hundreds of football books of every description dating back 100 years and more. Historical works, coaching manuals, popular annuals, press cuttings, minutes of F.A. meetings, football autobiographies — they are all there. And whisper it — even some cricket books, including a set of Wisdens.

In the Council Chambers, Graham Kelly examines another link with his Football League past. The painting — a crowd scene from the 1950's outside the Chelsea ground at Stamford Bridge — was presented to the F.A. by the Football League, to mark the Association's 90th Anniversary in 1953.

In the F.A.'s Council Chamber, where all the great decisions on the game's future are taken in meetings of the Council's 91 members.

A certificate presented to the Football Assocation by FIFA to mark England's qualification for the finals of the World Cup.

Another display of cups and trophies, souvenirs and gifts from around the world of football, including a replica of the Jules Rimet World Cup, won by England in 1966, and a ceramic version of the current World Cup trophy.

Graham Kelly with the painting presented to him on his departure from the Football League, by staff at Lytham St. Annes. The painting of Football League headquarters was done by the husband of one of the secretaries at the League offices.

The oak-panelled reception hall at Lancaster Gate, with its ornate, restored ceiling, and display cabinets.

PAUL STEWART *Spurs*

TOMMY COYNE *Celtic*

THOSE YO-YO YEARS!

That's the experience of Middlesbrough's
GARY PARKINSON

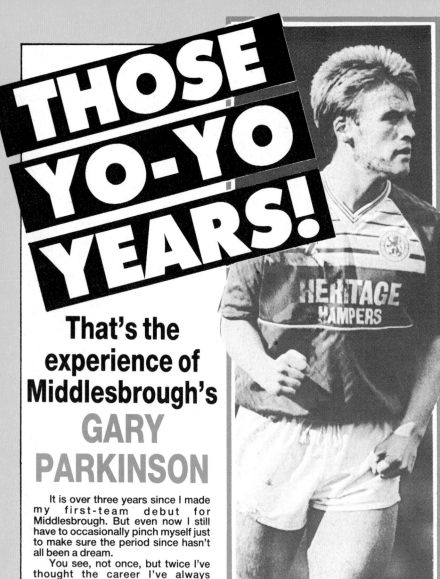

It is over three years since I made my first-team debut for Middlesbrough. But even now I still have to occasionally pinch myself just to make sure the period since hasn't all been a dream.

You see, not once, but twice I've thought the career I've always wanted in League football might be plucked from my grasp even before it had got off the ground.

The first was when I suffered the curse of so many youngsters who have to move away from family and friends for the first time... homesickness!

I was just 16 when I packed my bags and waved good-bye to Teesside to begin an apprenticeship with Everton. It was a day I'd waited two years for. But little did I realise the pitfalls that were to follow.

I'd had my first glimpse of Goodison Park as a schoolboy when I was invited down for trials. I'd fallen in love with the place straight away. Everton is a magnificent club. I couldn't wait to sign for them.

Within a couple of months of doing just that, however, the dream had turned into a nightmare. The football side of things was marvellous, but I couldn't settle off the field.

I'm not ashamed to admit that I missed the comforts of home, my family and friends. No matter how hard I tried I couldn't wait to get back to Teesside at every available opportunity.

Finally, I couldn't take any more and went to those in charge at Everton to explain just how unhappy

I'd become. I did so even in the knowledge that I might be scuppering any career I had in the game.

Fortunately, the folk at Everton couldn't have been more understanding. They didn't try to tell me I was being stupid or anything like that. Instead they showed great sympathy and agreed to cancel my apprenticeship so I could return home.

It was only when I was back on Teesside that I genuinely began to wonder where I went from there. An offer to team up with Fourth Division Darlington was about the best I had.

I was, in fact, on the very point of signing for them when my home-town club, Middlesbrough, suddenly offered me a place at Ayresome Park.

I could hardly believe my luck, especially as I had had the opportunity to join them as a schoolboy, but had passed up the chance because I had eyes only for Everton.

It was a break I hardly expected. For the next two years I was happy as a sandboy. That is till the world appeared set to not only cave in on me, but on the entire football club as well.

By this time I had signed full professional forms. But come the summer of '86 Boro' had not only been relegated to Division Three, but were in such dire financial straits that there was a very real threat that the club would be closed down.

The gates of the ground were locked, we had to train on public pitches, wash and iron our own training gear and for a spell didn't even pick up a weekly pay cheque.

I don't think I'll ever go through a more worrying period in my life again. The affair dragged on all summer and almost every day I feared the worst. Not just for the club but myself as well.

I was still only 18 at the time. Untried and unheard of, I didn't have one League appearance to my name and doubted if anyone else would be interested in me should the club eventually fold.

Right up till the very eve of the 1986-87 season, in fact, serious doubts about Boro' continuing in League football remained. It was only at the very last minute that we were given the go-head to kick off on opening day.

But even then things were hardly normal. Ayresome Park couldn't be made ready for our opening fixture against Port Vale. The match had to be played along the road at the Victoria Ground home of neighbouring Hartlepool.

It was also there on that day that my own personal fairytale began.

One minute I'd been wondering whether I still had a future in the game. The next I suddenly found myself plunged straight in at the deep-end as manager Bruce Rioch handed me my first-team debut.

Even today I can still hardly believe it happened. It was so unexpected. I just couldn't believe my luck. And, to be honest, in many ways I still can't.

I went on to become an ever-present in the line-up that season. Not only that, the club survived and recovered so well that I was part of a side that earned promotion back to the Second Division.

The following season I was again very much a regular as we did the promotion trick again and jumped all the way back to Division One and games against the Liverpools and Manchester Uniteds of this world.

Our spell in the top flight, however, lasted just one season. The end of the 1988-89 term saw us relegated. It was a shattering blow — but, if there's one thing the last few years have taught me, it's that in football you have to accept the ups and downs.

Because of my own experiences I'm always very appreciative of what the game has given me. But the last thing I'll ever be guilty of is getting carried away by it all.

That's why I never take anything for granted. Mine is still very much a policy of taking each and every game as it comes. You just never know what's waiting round the corner. My career so far is the proof of that!

TREVOR PUTNEY *Norwich*

DOUBLING UP SUITS ME!

BLACKBURN ROVERS' TERRY GENNOE EXPLAINS

TERRY GENNOE is leading a double life. He's a footballer — and a schoolteacher.

The Blackburn Rovers goalkeeper went part-time at the start of last season and now splits his week. Three days on the training field with his Ewood Park team-mates are combined with two days on the playing fields of a local secondary school.

Gennoe, who a couple of years ago collected a degree in biology by studying an Open University course in his spare time, coupled promotion fighting with the teaching of lacrosse, badminton and virtually every other sport.

He explains, "In the summer of 1988 I had to have an operation on my knee. It was caused by wear and tear and had been building up over the years.

"Afterwards the specialist advised me that the knee would stand up better if I cut down on my training. I should take two days off each week. Work for just three days instead of five.

"That gave me spare time and I decided to make good use of it. I applied for a job as a Physical Education teacher and got it.

"At first, my manager at Blackburn, Don Mackay, was worried that I was taking on something which might affect my game adversely.

"I assured him the club would still come first. If, for instance, we had a midweek game which cut across my regular days at the school — Wednesday and Thursday — it would be the teaching which took second place.

"I also agreed that if he felt my form was suffering, I'd give up the work at school. However, the exact opposite happened. Far from losing form, I actually played as well last season as I had in any of my previous 15 campaigns in the game.

"I felt mentally fresh and sharp. Physically I felt very fit. I put both down to the fact I was splitting my week between the two jobs."

Terry continues, "You can become a little stale going out on to the same training pitch week after week, year after year. The break exercised my mind in other directions as well as reducing the workload on my knee.

"I'm having to swot up on sports about which I don't have a comprehensive knowledge. I'll go to the library perhaps on a Monday afternoon and do my research. I have lesson notes to compile, too.

"I can specialise in football coaching, of course, but I cover many other sports, too. I teach rugby, volleyball, lacrosse, athletics, badminton, cricket, tennis . . . the lot.

"It really has given me a new lease of life. I thoroughly like my teaching and I'm now enjoying my football as much as at any time in the last 16 years.

"I intend to stay in the game as long as I physically can," he goes on. "For now, I'm quite happy to divide my energies between Rovers and the school. But there will obviously have to come a time when I seriously think about going into teaching on a permanent basis.

"Then I will probably face a dilemma. I shall have to decide whether to carry on as a Physical Education teacher, trained as I am in secondary education or to be a general teacher, perhaps in a primary school.

"The PE is fine just now, but it's hard to visualise me running out in my tracksuit when I'm 60! I may decide to do more work in the classroom. I've already tried my hand at it and it is something I'm sure I'd get a lot out of."

Meanwhile, Terry is hoping for a final flourish in the First Division before swapping his gloves for a blackboard and chalk.

"The way last season went for me, I've no doubts in my own mind I can do a good job in the top flight," he ends. "Keeping goal is just about stopping the ball going into the net. That doesn't alter, whatever division you are playing in."

NIGEL CLOUGH
Nottingham Forest

THE next time you see a club physiotherapist running on to the field to assist a hurt player, consider the skill and knowledge being put to use in assessing and treating the injury.

There's a lot more to being the "sponge man" than meets the eye. The days of using the cold sponge to treat everything are gone. I know, because I've just completed a two-part physiotherapy course which, hopefully, will enable me to do that job when my playing career comes to an end.

I can tell you the work that went into the course was the hardest I've ever done in my life.

But it was all worth it. Now I can concentrate on my football knowing that I have made a solid step towards securing my future.

The Football Association has ruled that, by 1990, the medical man at every League club must be a fully qualified chartered physiotherapist, or has been registered with the League as having completed the FA's own course — the one which I have been through.

But why did I want to be a physio when most players who intend to remain in the game do so in a coaching or managerial capacity?

That goes back ten years to my days as a Shrewsbury Town player. Following a knee injury, I had to have a cartilage removed, and the post-operative process involved attending Shrewsbury Hospital as an out-patient.

For ten weeks I was put through a full physiotherapy programme, ensuring that every move I made was the right one at the right time.

Later, I realised just how lucky I was that my club, and particularly the physio, Derek Mann, arranged for me to attend.

In the past few years, I have known players who were treated on the pitch by unqualified physios. There have been some who were sent back into action with broken legs when they shouldn't have been moved, and the decision has cost them their careers. That's why the new ruling by the FA is such an important one.

My own course of treatment had another long-term effect. During those weeks of reporting every day to the hospital, I became fascinated with the way my recovery had been mapped out for me.

My own recovery, coupled with the chance to watch the way in which other patients were

THE COLD SPONGE

helped, made me decide that this was what I wanted to do in the future.

So, when I discovered I could take a three-year Chartered Physiotherapy course at Lilleshall, I enrolled.

I undertook the first year, which consisted of a week's intensive tuition during the summer of 1981, followed by a year of hard work at home.

I had the help of a fellow student, Clement McBride, an army PT instructor who looked after Shrewsbury's junior players on a part-time basis. We spent hours in each other's homes, helping one another study.

Derek Mann was also a great help. He set impromptu tests for me. For example, I might arrive for training one morning and, in front of the rest of the team, he'd ask me to name all the muscles in the lower leg.

In February of that season, however, I was shattered to discover that the course was being scrapped.

The Football Association had earmarked Lilleshall as the base for their new School of Excellence and Rehabilitation Centre. While all the work was being done to prepare the centre, there was no room for the course.

A year or so later, however, I discovered that the FA were planning to launch their own physiotherapy course at Lilleshall.

This was to be a two-year programme and they were specifically looking for League players to enrol. Consequently, I arrived in the summer of 1988 to begin my studies all over again.

It was the most exhausting fortnight of my life. A residential course, our day started when we rose at 7.30, and we were in the classroom before nine o'clock.

That first half of the course concentrated on the lower part of the body, and the classroom part of the schedule consisted of lectures by a number of guest specialists.

These would be consultants from London or Birmingham who specialised in particular fields, but who were used to treating injured footballers.

Lunch was from noon until two o'clock, when we reported back for another three and a half hours of instruction.

Though we did some classroom work in the afternoon, this would be broken up by periods when we went out to the pitch for practical demonstrations.

A further hour and a half was set apart for an evening meal before we were back in the classroom for more lectures.

Even at the end of that, however, the day wasn't finished. Everyone would probably relax together for about an hour before we retired to our rooms.

But the course was so demanding that we still needed to spend several hours studying on our own. I was up until about two o'clock every morning with my nose buried in books.

At the end of the fortnight, there was a written exam and a practical test. A passmark was essential in order to qualify for the second part of the course in the summer of 1989. Of 26 class members, 24 were successful.

But, of course, there was no point in forgetting about the course until we reported a year later.

We knew that there would be a revision exam on the first day. We were also told that the second part, dealing with the upper part of the body, was much tougher. So we'd have to

spend a lot of time during the year in intense preparation.

Gordon Guthrie, the Derby County physio, has been a great help. He has allowed me to visit his treatment room and watch him in action, and he has been happy to answer all the questions I fire at him.

DURING that year, I was sent a regular supply of work and study sheets, and book lists. It was a hard time for my wife Helen, and our two young sons.

After getting the boys off to bed, it wasn't unusual for me to spend three hours locked away in study during the evening, leaving Helen to sit on her own.

But she was a marvellous help. While I trained in the morning, she'd be scouring the bookshops to find the volumes I needed. She'd also assist if there was a particular chapter I was having difficulty in learning.

Overall, it has been a tough programme, but it has also given me a lot of satisfaction.

I'm now looking to gain further qualifications. Graham Smith, the resident physio at Lilleshall, has been trying to set up a third part of the course which will lead to the Chartered Physiotherapists Association recognising us.

Though our completion of the FA course is sufficient to meet their standard, and we have a good working knowledge of the subject, our qualifications are not as high as a student who has gone through a Chartered Physios course.

Danny Thomas, the former Spurs player, for example, has been studying the subject at college. That's a full-time course lasting three years.

Since we've spent only four weeks' full-time study, it's understandable that the CPA have found it difficult to accept us. One way or another, I'd like to take my studies further.

DAYS ARE GONE!

ACTION SPECIAL! --ACTION SPECIAL! --ACT

Norwich City goalkeeper **BRYAN GUNN** rises to the occasion to beat off the challenge of Middlesbrough's **TONY MOWBRAY.**

KELLY'S COLOURS

If all the laundry ladies at the 92 League clubs pooled together the amount of playing kit they see in a week, they still couldn't match the number with which John Kelly can surround himself on his days off from Oldham Athletic.

When the 28-year-old midfielder's commitments with the Second Division club allow, John is a director and working member of a growing family business in football kit manufacturing.

The hub of the Kelly operation is their Liverpool showroom where around 10,000 items of soccer gear are housed awaiting distribution throughout the UK.

John's father began the business with a sports shop in Liverpool 25 years ago when he quit the game after a career with Arsenal and Nottingham Forest.

Paul Kelly expanded the idea four years ago with the help of brother John by venturing into the massive nationwide market.

Now many of the amateur clubs playing in Leagues in the north on a Saturday and Sunday have their kit supplied by the Kelly firm.

Shirts, shorts, socks, bibs and tracksuits in a variety of colours are available and the proud boast is that they can have any order delivered anywhere in the country within 72 hours!

John's contacts in the football world have helped promote the business. He even persuaded Everton and Wales captain Kevin Ratcliffe to do a spot of modelling for the catalogue!

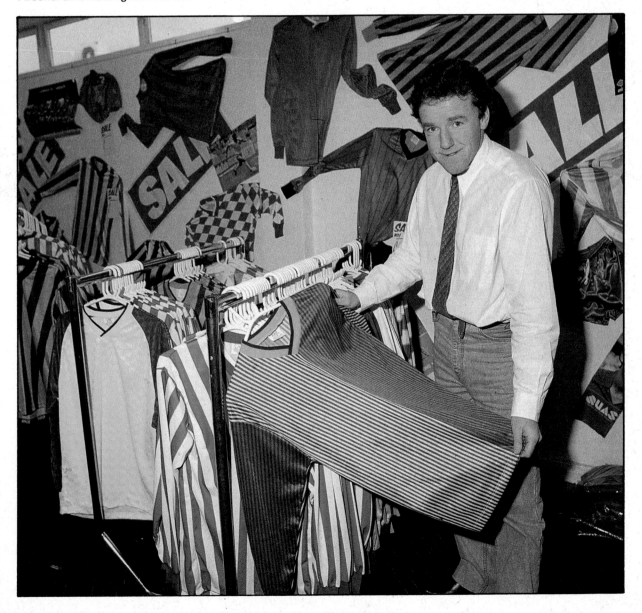

TAKING OVER WAS TOUGH!

HANS SEGERS talks about his move

to Wimbledon to replace local hero

DAVE BEASANT.

I KNEW that I was taking on a tough challenge when I took over as goalkeeper at Wimbledon. Because the man I was replacing was Dave Beasant.

A few months before I went to Plough Lane, Wimbledon beat Liverpool at Wembley to win the F.A. Cup. Dave was the captain that day and he was also the hero. A TV audience of millions saw him make several great saves including the memorable one from John Aldridge's penalty.

That was the act that I had to follow when I signed from Nottingham Forest. Manager Bobby Gould made it quite clear what he expected from his last line of defence. At Wimbledon the 'keeper was the most important player in the team because everything started from him.

I quickly had to get used to a style of play completely different to that at Nottingham Forest. There, my first option was usually to throw the ball out to a defender, but it was to be different now.

Dave Beasant had always made very good use of his long kicks and I had to make sure that mine were up to the mark. He would also come out of the penalty area to play the ball and I had to master that as well. It took a few weeks to settle down but I soon felt comfortable with the new things I was doing.

I'd thought it might take a long time for the fans to forget big Dave. After all, he had been there since the club was in the Fourth Division. But thankfully the supporters seemed to take to me pretty quickly.

But the most important thing for me at that stage was that I was back playing first-team football. That had not been the story in my last couple of seasons at Forest, when Steve Sutton kept me out of the side.

I had started to think that I might have to look elsewhere in Europe for a new club, having started my career at P.S.V. Eindhoven in my home country Holland. I even went to Belgium to talk to a couple of clubs. Then one day I got a call from Nottingham Forest to say that Bobby Gould wanted to talk to me about a possible move to Wimbledon.

I wasn't quite sure about moving to a London club but Bobby Gould managed to persuade me that the capital was the place to start the next step of my career in English football.

When I was a kid growing up in Holland I had always dreamt about playing in England because I knew it had such a good league. Even when I started playing for a top club like P.S.V. Eindhoven I knew that one day I would want to move on to England.

There were only a few top clubs in Holland, so Ajax, Feyenoord, and P.S.V. won most of the trophies between them. Even now, though we have a strong national team, the league isn't very competitive. Nobody seems to be able to stop P.S.V. winning the league these days.

I had seen Arnold Muhren and Frans Thijssen both do very well in England playing for Ipswich, and I was keen to follow their example.

I finally got my chance when my fellow countryman Hans Van Breukelen joined P.S.V. after a spell in England with Nottingham Forest. We trained together for a few weeks and during that time he told me all about life with Forest; about the team, the manager Brian Clough, the city and the good places to live.

It didn't take too much convincing by Hans for me to want to join Forest. He phoned the club on my behalf and luckily his recommendation got me the move I wanted.

The first couple of years at the City Ground went very well for me even though the team weren't winning trophies. I knew that I was learning a lot about the game by playing against English teams.

Things only started to go wrong when Steve Sutton took over from me as first choice 'keeper. He played so well that there was no way back for me. I found myself stuck in the reserves and that's no good for anyone, especially a goalkeeper.

STEVE SUTTON

It became particularly frustrating for me when I saw P.S.V. win the European Cup by beating Benfica and then a few weeks later, Holland won the European championships in West Germany. That made me think how much I would like to play for Holland myself. When I was a youngster I played in representative matches with the likes of Ruud Gullit and Marco Van Basten. I'd very much like to establish myself in the Dutch squad in time for the 1990 World Cup.

Of course, they've been drawn in a very tough qualifying group with West Germany, Wales and Finland but they should make it to Italy in 1990.

Perhaps I'll be able to get a place in the squad alongside my old friend Hans Van Breukelen.

I feel that I should now be coming to my peak as a goalkeeper and I'd like to show that at international level.

As far as club football is concerned I'm committed to Wimbledon for the next three years. After that I'll have to decide what I want to do next. Perhaps I'll move to where I can use another of my languages.

When I came to England I spoke only schoolboy English. But, of course, a few years in this country have been a big help to my wife and myself. We've also been able to bring up our children to speak two languages. Dutch is the first language at home but it's usually English everywhere else. My little girl switches quite happily from one to another.

I suppose as the children get older we will have to decide where we want them to be educated. That might be back home in Holland, or here in England, or perhaps somewhere else.

Last season I found myself using a third language when I went to the Wimbledon training ground. This came about when Bobby Gould signed midfielder Detzi Kruszynski. I was to be the interpreter for the new man. I must admit that for a long time I thought he was a German because that was the language we spoke, but then I discovered he was actually Polish!

My German isn't up to the mark of my English but it was good enough to pass on tactical messages to Detzi. But thankfully football is a universal language so he soon picked up what was happening.

I have also learnt a bit of Spanish in the past so perhaps Bobby will buy somebody from Real Madrid so that I can practise!

Whatever happens in the future, I'm glad I took on the challenge of stepping into Dave Beasant's shoes at Wimbledon.

DAVID ROCASTLE
Arsenal

TEAMWORK!

Nottingham Forest's STUART PEARCE (left) and COLIN FOSTER join forces to clear their lines.

MARK STEIN *Queen's Park Rangers*

HANG ON!

Nottingham Forest defender **DES WALKER** makes sure he keeps a firm hold on Luton's **MICK HARFORD.**

43

Mr. Middlesbrough!

For as long as he can remember, David Moles has been a Middlesbrough fan. He never misses a game, home or away, and he reckons he spends £30 every week on papers and materials to keep up-to-date his own records of the club.

But an even more amazing example of David's devotion to his favourite club is the fact that on 31st January, 1989, he had his name changed by deed poll to David Bernie Bruce Middlesbrough. Bernie and Bruce being the Christian names of Bernie Slaven, his favourite player, and Bruce Rioch, the Middlesbrough manager!

KEVIN DRINKELL
Rangers

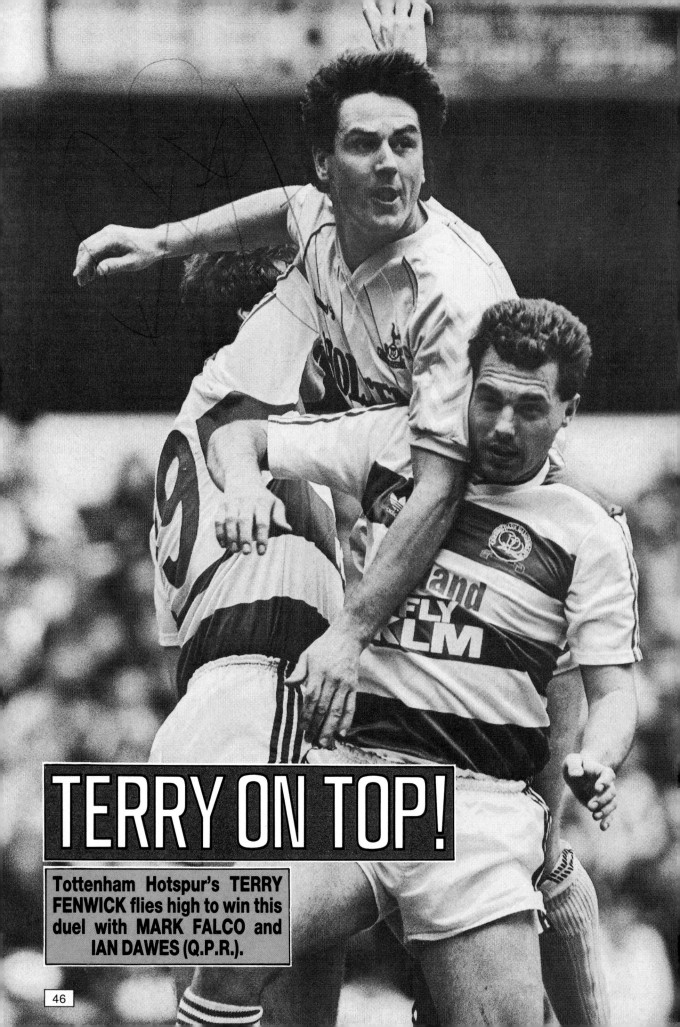

TERRY ON TOP!

Tottenham Hotspur's TERRY FENWICK flies high to win this duel with MARK FALCO and IAN DAWES (Q.P.R.).

NIGEL PEARSON *Sheffield Wednesday*

47

FRANZ CARR
Nottingham Forest

JOHN BARNES *Liverpool*

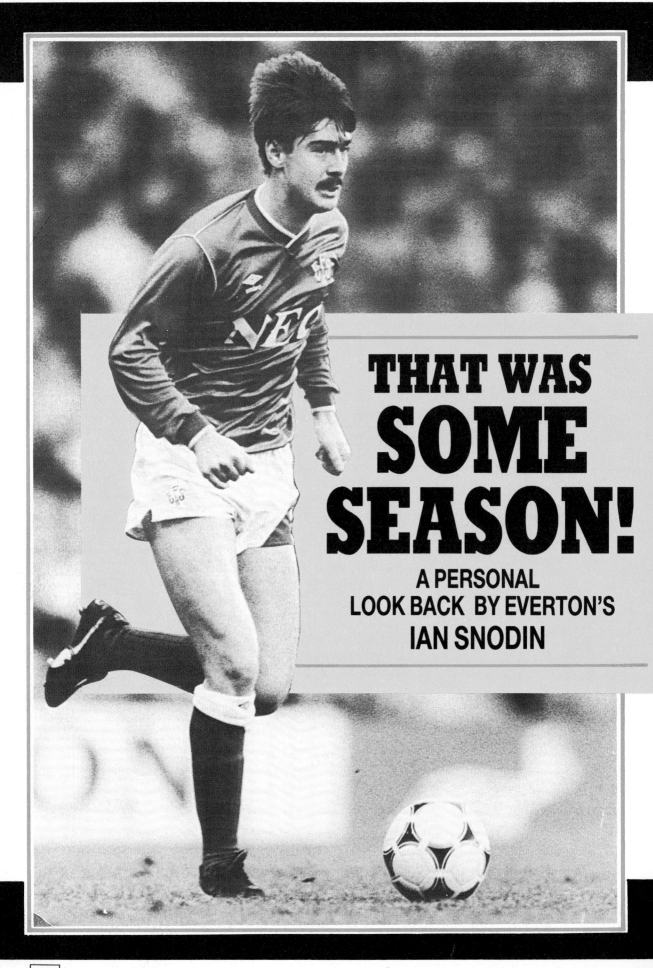

THAT WAS SOME SEASON!

A PERSONAL LOOK BACK BY EVERTON'S IAN SNODIN

It's been a topsy-turvy year for Ian Snodin. The Everton star has had a busy time of it on the club front, filling three different roles whilst fighting off injury problems.

And if that isn't enough, Ian has also made the break into the full England squad in a completely unaccustomed role. Here we take a peep inside Ian's diary and find out just what has made up this most hectic of seasons.

1988

AUGUST 2:

Ian flies out to Switzerland for a pre-season tour as an emergency defender because of injuries to Kevin Ratcliffe and Pat Van den Hauwe. Still on Everton's books despite paper talk linking him with a move to Sheffield Wednesday, something that hadn't entered his mind.

"I didn't even speak to Wednesday. In fact it was never my intention to leave Everton."

AUGUST 27:

Everton start their season with a fine 4-0 win over Newcastle. Snodin plays in the centre of defence and his performance is hailed as "brilliant" by manager Colin Harvey. The role is nothing new to the increasingly versatile Yorkshireman.

"Injuries left us without cover at the back and when the boss heard I'd played there for Doncaster and Leeds, I was handed the job.

"I'm enjoying it. I find I have more time to weigh things up and, when I do get into tricky situations, my pace generally takes me out of them."

OCTOBER 8:

Dave Watson and Kevin Ratcliffe are both fit again for the visit of Southampton. Ian is switched to right-back — unfamiliar territory.

"The day before the game the manager came to me and told me I'd be switching. I'd never played there in my life before, not even in a practice match or training."

NOVEMBER 26:

Following some impressive displays in the number two jersey, Ian is watched by England boss Bobby Robson in a game at West Ham. Colin Harvey, the Everton manager, declares "Ian is the best right-back in England at the moment."

DECEMBER 17:

Another trip to the capital and again Bobby Robson is a spectator at the 0-0 draw with Queen's Park Rangers. Asked about Snodin's international chances, Robson replies, "He is at the right age and could be a possibility for me in the future. All he has to do now is learn a bit more positional sense at full-back."

1989

JANUARY 31:

The long-awaited international call-up arrives with Ian selected for England's friendly in Greece.

"It's everyone's ambition to play for their country and I hope things will go on from here. I could have left Everton in the summer but I decided to stay and fight for a place. I never thought it would come to this — picked as a full-back in the England squad."

That same night, however, things turn sour for Ian. He is injured in Everton's FA cup replay victory over Plymouth.

FEBRUARY 4:

The hamstring problem picked up in the FA cup tie rules Snodin out of the home encounter with Wimbledon. It also forces his withdrawal from the England party due to fly out to Athens the next day.

FEBRUARY 18:

Back in action and a return to midfield for another FA cup game. This time it's away to Barnsley and both Ian and Everton come away from Oakwell unscathed.

FEBRUARY 24:

Relief for Ian as he is named in the England squad for the crucial World Cup qualifier in Albania.

"I'm delighted to be included again and I'm looking forward to being on the trip this time.

"With not going to Greece I did begin to wonder if I would be picked for this one, because after all it is a crucial World Cup game."

MARCH 8:

England secure a 2-0 win over their Albanian hosts. Ian views proceedings from the stand, not selected in the starting eleven or as a substitute — although he didn't expect to be.

"The first time is really a case of seeing what it's all about, but once you've got a taste, you want more.

"It was an important game and the manager was bound to go with his senior players, but I enjoyed the experience ."

MARCH 11:

Back to League action and to the right-back spot, but it isn't a happy return. Ian is carried off with a hamstring injury — the left leg this time — in the 31st minute of the game with Sheffield Wednesday.

"You'd have thought I had done enough running about in half an hour to be alright, but I chased a long ball and suddenly had to pull up. I was in a fair bit of pain and it was quite sore when I was in the nursing home for three or four days' rest."

APRIL 1:

The home game with Queen's Park Rangers is the fifth Ian has missed because of the injury.

"When I was first injured, I'd have settled to be in the state I am now. It's certainly feeling easier than I expected at this stage."

Colin Harvey, however, wasn't quite as optimistic when he said "Ian Snodin is making steady progress but it's still too early to assess when he might be ready to play again."

MAY 3:

Merseyside takes its first step back towards normality after the Hillsborough tragedy with the Everton v Liverpool 'derby' match at Goodison.

Having returned from the FA's rehabilitation centre at Lilleshall just two days before, Ian is only a spectator. As far as first-team football is concerned, Ian's season is over. Although it's a sad way to end, season 1988-89 will be one that Ian Snodin will never forget.

FLAT OUT — BUT HE CAN STILL RAISE A SMILE!

Norwich City goalkeeper Bryan Gunn has hit the deck — but he can still find something to smile about!

STEVE FOSTER *Luton*

WHY I LEFT

QUEEN'S PARK RANGERS' NIGEL SPACKMAN EXPLAINS.

LIVERPOOL!

I BELIEVE that footballers should have a strong say in what happens to our game. I've always thought it was important for players to take a part in the leadership of the game.

That's why I have so enjoyed the time that I have spent on the committee of the Professional Footballers' Association. It's an important time for players to be involved in the direction that football is taking.

I did stand in the election for Chairman of the P.F.A., but the vote went to Garth Crooks, and I was very happy for him to be chosen. Garth is a very good ambassador for the game, and I try to give him all the help I can.

I feel I have a role to play off the pitch as well as on it. I always like to have a chat with players from other clubs to compare the challenges and problems that we face as professional footballers.

Obviously, those problems are very different between the top First Division sides and the Fourth Division clubs, and I'm always interested to hear the views of players lower down the league.

I've had experience of being with the best — at Liverpool — and with a non-league club, Andover, as well as with teams in between such as Bournemouth, Chelsea and Queen's Park Rangers.

One day I would like to put everything I've learned to good use as a manager or a coach. But, for the time being, actually playing the game is the most important thing. It's no good being able to talk about football if you can't do your stuff on the pitch.

And I aim to do just that for a few years yet, with Q.P.R. I see it as a very exciting period for the club. It's a good time to have joined Rangers, because the potential is tremendous.

Having said that, I've got to admit that it was tough for me last season to leave Anfield. It wasn't a decision I wanted to make. I don't believe any player who has done well for Liverpool ever wants to leave. Not many players who have left Anfield have been as successful elsewhere. I've got to aim to reverse the trend — and I think I can do it with Rangers.

It was a question of what was best for my career in the long term. It was a tough choice. Did I stay at Anfield, where I was stuck in the reserves, and fight to regain a first-team place? Or did I move on to a new challenge with Rangers who obviously had big ambitions?

Q.P.R.'s manager, Trevor Francis, persuaded me that the only choice was to join Rangers. I was impressed by Trevor.

He was determined to put together a very good side at Loftus Road. When he was talking to me, he also had plans to sign Andy Gray from Aston Villa, and Peter Reid from Everton. Later on he was to get striker Colin Clarke from Southampton.

I had become used to playing alongside top quality players at Liverpool, and I realised it would be very similar at Rangers. The most interesting part for me, was the prospect of linking up with Peter Reid. We had a lot of good midfield battles when I was at Liverpool, and he was with Everton.

It was always a tremendous challenge to try to get the better of Peter and his colleagues. Those Merseyside derby games were the highlights of my two years at Anfield.

Matches against Everton were always fantastic occasions, the atmosphere like a cup final. It was ironic that the year Everton won the championship from under our noses, we beat them 3-1 to get revenge. But the season we walked away with the league, Everton was the team to end our fantastic unbeaten run.

I would never have guessed that I'd end up playing alongside Peter Reid. But it was an added incentive to join Rangers, when I knew Tevor Francis was trying to get him to join as well.

Playing alongside such an experienced internationalist as Peter made it a lot easier to settle in at Rangers. Like all Liverpool and Everton players, we got to know each other well on Merseyside, and on joining Q.P.R. we were determined to do a good job together.

It must have been as tough for Peter Reid to leave Everton, as it was for me to quit Liverpool. Perhaps tougher, because he was there much longer. Two years was really not long enough for me at Anfield. But I still count myself lucky to have had the chance to play there at all.

It had come as a big surprise to learn that Kenny Dalglish wanted to sign me. I was at Chelsea, and I didn't have a clue that he was watching me. But when the chance came up, I couldn't say no to the opportunity. I

knew all along that I could never be sure about a first-team place, but it was worth a shot.

I joined at a very exciting stage of the season. Having done the double the previous season, Liverpool were in the hunt to do it again.

My debut was actually in a Littlewoods Cup semi-final second leg against Southampton. I came on as a sub in a game we won 3-0, so right away I had the prospect of a Wembley final to look forward to.

In fact, I stayed in the side for the rest of the season — which turned into an anti-climax in some ways. We lost the Littlewoods final to Arsenal, after leading 1-0, and Everton snatched the league title.

But those disappointments couldn't dampen my spirits. It felt great just to be wearing the famous red strip. The end of the season came all too quickly for me — and then I found out how tough it was to hold down a regular place with a team like Liverpool.

I didn't make it into the starting line-up the next season, and that was to count against me. The team started off like an express train, and although I got the occasional game here and there, I wasn't a regular.

It wasn't a good time to be missing out. The team were on a long unbeaten run which lasted until the Everton match in March — 29 matches in all. It looked as if I was going to be permanently stuck on the subs' bench, but in January I came in for Ronnie Whelan, and stayed in for the rest of the season.

What a team that was! Peter Beardsley, John Barnes, John Aldridge and Ray Houghton were ripping sides apart up front. And the rest of the team was in very special form as well. It was a privilege to be part of such a side.

The shock was losing to Wimbledon in the F.A. Cup final. Nobody expected that. It just proves you can't take anything for granted, even at Liverpool.

Perhaps I should have said 'particularly at a club like Liverpool'. Because you can't guarantee a place at Anfield from one week to the next. There are too many good players.

I found myself out of the side again at the start of last season. And this time I wasn't so happy just to wait and fight for a place. Things were not going well for the team. There were a lot of injuries. I believed I was worth a regular place.

Sitting on the subs' bench during the 'live' T.V. match against Arsenal, I suddenly came to the decision that I would have to leave Anfield to re-establish myself as a first-team player.

It wasn't long before I was signing on for Rangers — to be followed by Peter Reid within a few days.

I believe that what we learned on Merseyside can help Queen's Park Rangers challenge our former clubs for supremacy. We will certainly do our best to see that it does.

PETER REID

GARY CROSBY *Nottingham Forest*

RICHARD GOUGH *Rangers*

THE LOWDOWN ON WOLVES' HIGH-FLYING STRIKER *STEVE BULL*

Mr. GOALS!

1

When West Bromwich Albion signed him, he was earning £27 a week as a factory worker and playing Sunday football — "I never felt I would become a professional footballer," he says.

2

Played seven times for West Brom, scoring three goals. "When the manager at the time — Ron Saunders — told me Wolves had made a £50,000 bid for me I thought to myself, 'I'm never worth that.'"

STEVE BULL — Caught by the camera on his debut for the England Under-21 side against Albania.

3

On his future — "I'm a local lad playing for my local team and I think the way things are going Wolves will eventually be as big as anything in the First Division."

FACTS & FIGURES

First season at Wolves — 33 games, 18 goals.
Second season — 58 games, 52 goals.
Third season — 55 games, 49 goals.
Eleven hat-tricks.
Best run: 12 goals in five matches between November 26 and December 17, 1988.
Longest run without a goal: Four matches. (September 1988).

WHAT THEY SAY ABOUT STEVE . . .

Graham Turner (Wolves manager) — "Steve is the most exciting player I've ever worked with because every time he gets the ball I feel he is going to score."

Don Howe (England Assistant Manager) — "He is willing to work tirelessly, making endless runs into the penalty area to get into shooting positions. But most important of all, he is single-minded. He just wants to get the ball where it should be — in the net."

John Richards (former Wolves striker) — "Steve and his partner Andy Mutch have a relationship with the crowd that hasn't been seen at Molineux since Derek Dougan and myself were playing up front. They score more than we did. It may have been in the lower divisions, but even at that level we wouldn't have got near the sort of figures they have achieved."

Alan McInally (Aston Villa) — "Steve's scoring record speaks volumes for his ability. His strength helps him get past defenders and he has the perfect finishing touch."

Alan Smith (Arsenal) — "Bull is a player who goes after the ball around the box. And he has a good accurate shot when he gets it. If he can do the same thing at higher levels he will be a sensation."

Keith Edwards (Hull City's 200-plus goal striker) — "Bull has the fantastic scoring knack. What a scoring average. If he scores at that rate in the Second Division he would be worth the £1.7 million Spurs paid Manchester City for Paul Stewart."

Garry Birtles (Notts County) — "He is quick, strong and takes some stopping in front of goal. These are big assets at any level. I'm sure it would work for him in the First."

KERRY DIXON *Chelsea*

KEVIN MOORE *Southampton*

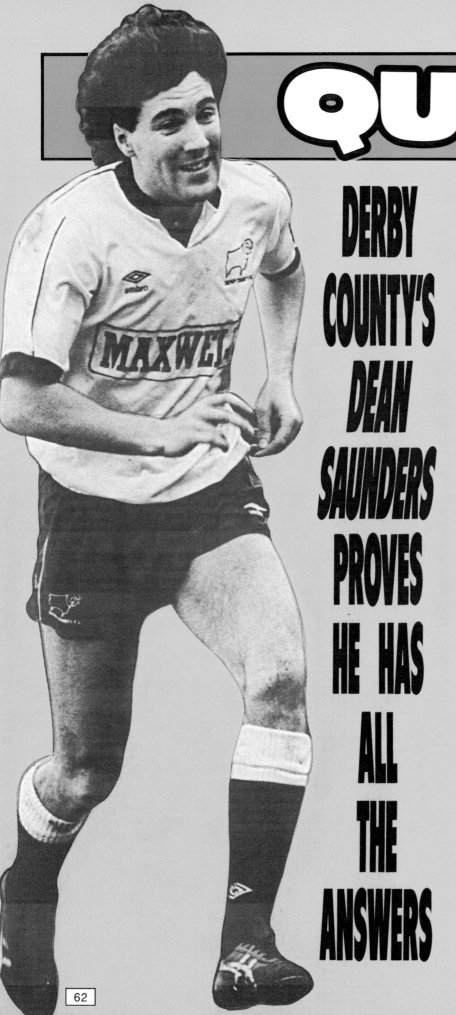

QUEST

DERBY COUNTY'S DEAN SAUNDERS PROVES HE HAS ALL THE ANSWERS

IN October, 1988, Dean Saunders moved from Oxford United to Derby County for £1 million. How did the big money move affect the goal-hungry striker? Dean Saunders himself gives the answers.

What made you choose Derby County?

On the face of it, the advantage was obvious. I was moving from a Second Division club to one in the First.

But, apart from knowing that Derby were a big club whose honours list included the League Championship, the real yardstick I used was the quality of players already there. I figured that, if Derby was good enough for top names such as Peter Shilton and Mark Wright, then it had to be good enough for me.

Did you feel the pressure of your million pound transfer fee?

I knew that at the first suggestion I wasn't living up to my price tag, I would be criticised. But I made it a lot easier for myself by scoring goals as soon as I pulled on a Derby jersey.

Of course, there's no way I could have kept up the scoring rate which I achieved in my first few weeks at the Baseball Ground. At one stage I had seven goals from six matches.

All I could do was keep it up for as long as I could, and accept it when my goals began to ease off.

When that did happen, I was able to relax. I'd successfully come through the most testing first few weeks.

For one thing, while I was scoring and we were winning matches, the County fans were being won over to my side. By the time I went a few games without finding the target, there was little chance of them barracking me.

What sort of an influence has manager Arthur Cox had on you?

I don't think I've ever been kept on my toes as much as I have at Derby. Arthur Cox has seen to that. His influence has helped me become a better player than I was when he signed me.

For one thing, he's never satisfied with my performances, and doesn't want me to be satisfied either.

He keeps giving me videos of Derby matches to study. The idea is that I watch my own

ARTHUR COX

performances, pick out situations which I could have handled better, and work at improving them.

Nothing is said afterwards. He simply expects I'll spot the same things he has done and that I'll be putting the lessons into practice on the field.

What did you find was the biggest difference between playing for Derby and your previous club Oxford?

It's the first time I've played for a club which can boast such a solid defence. Having that strength behind you provides a big incentive for a striker.

I know, for instance, that whenever I score, the chances are that my goal will actually count towards taking points

from the match.

At Oxford, our defence wasn't so reliable. Many of my strikes ended up as consolation goals in games that we lost. After a while, that becomes depressing.

Your striking partner with Derby is Paul Goddard. How has that worked out?

We've not had as much chance as I would have liked to perfect that partnership. Paul had a lot of injury problems last season and struggled to string a run of games together. But he is a class player, and I'm convinced this link-up will work well.

It's a different type of pairing to others I've been used to, but as so often in the past, I'm fortunate to have such a good partner. At previous clubs, I played alongside Justin Fashanu, Mick Ferguson, Alan Biley, Alan Curtis, Bob Latchford, Ian Walsh and Billy Whitehurst.

Most were big players who were good in the air and were used as target men. I probably acquired my sharpness in front of goal by snapping up all the half-chances that they left for me.

With Paul Goddard it's different. We do a lot of running for each other and see ourselves as creators as well as scorers.

Last season saw you become a regular member of the Welsh international side. Was that a big boost to you?

It certainly was. It's not been easy to win a regular spot, as I'm competing with Mark Hughes and Ian Rush for the striking roles. But I'm certain there's a future for all three of us in the same side. Manager Terry Yorath has indicated that he could be of the same mind, having fielded all three of us in several games.

What we must do is start

banging in goals regularly to prove that the three-way partnership works. At least I've been given a chance and have something to keep plugging away for.

You now have one First Division season with Derby under your belt. How do you see the future?

From a personal point of view, I'm looking for an even better season this time. Though I settled into the Derby team fairly quickly, we moved into our new house only last June.

Staying in hotels, then rented accommodation, on top of having a new baby to look after, was a strain for my wife, and I felt some of it too. We're much happier in our own place.

On the club front, I'm optimistic about our chances of winning something.

Four times last season, we were poised to move into the top three had we taken three points from our next match.

On each occasion we lost — and two of those were to Luton Town and West Ham who were at the bottom of the table.

Had we taken full points we could have been involved in the title race until the end.

This time, I believe we are capable of taking a genuine shot at the Championship.

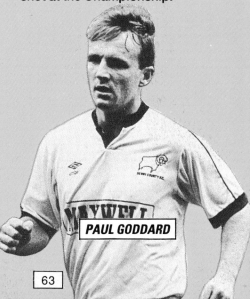

PAUL GODDARD

LLOYD McGRATH *Coventry*

PAT BONNER
Celtic

FULL STRETCH!

Aston Villa's **STEVE SIMS** finds those extra inches to get the better of Manchester United's **MARK HUGHES.**

COLIN PATES *Charlton*

BANANAS!

FOLLOW the inflatable banana — and you'll almost certainly find a Manchester City supporter.

Banana mania first hit Maine Road back in 1987. What started as a bit of a gimmick by just a few fans soon spread through the ranks.

Now it's just not bananas — there are dozens of different inflatables to be seen on the terraces, ranging from Frankenstein to paddling pools.

Now the craze has caught on with supporters of other clubs, but Manchester City fans still boast proudly that they were first to go bananas!

TONY COTTEE
Everton

Peter Nicholas (Chelsea)

FOOTBALL was just about the last thing on my mind when I agreed to join Chelsea last year. My little baby boy, just a few weeks old, was seriously ill, and had to spend a lot of time in hospital with my wife. My main consideration was finding a club near London that was convenient to my in-laws, who could take care of my other three children.

So you can appreciate how thrilled I am that things have worked out so well, with promotion being achieved in my first season at Stamford Bridge. I've played for two of the biggest clubs in Britain — Arsenal and Aberdeen — but I'm sure that Chelsea have the potential to be just as great a power in the game.

I was disappointed that my family crisis forced me to leave Aberdeen. And a few years ago I was equally disappointed that my spell with Arsenal was not more successful. But now I have no regrets at leaving either team. Success with Chelsea will be just as satisfying. It can become again one of the biggest clubs in the game.

Aberdeen had given me the chance to play in a very competitive league, and in European competition.

But when my son was ill, I had to put him first, and forget about football interests. I needed to get back to the London area, so I had to see which English teams were interested.

Several clubs approached me and it was nice to know that a few managers still had confidence in my ability. But one club stood out from the pack — Chelsea.

They had just been relegated from the First Division, there had been a lot of internal unrest, and the club seemed to be in a terrible state — but that didn't put me off.

I knew that Chelsea had a future, if the players could get it

GED DAYS AT CHELSEA!

together on the pitch. And after discussions with manager Bobby Campbell, I was convinced the club wouldn't stay long in the Second Division.

Around the same time as I signed, Graham Roberts, who had also been in Scotland with Glasgow Rangers, was having talks at Stamford Bridge. He, too, recognised the potential at Chelsea.

Between us, we decided we could play a big part in putting Chelsea back on its feet. Even so, when I first met up with the Chelsea players for training, I could tell that things were not right. The players had lost all belief in themselves after relegation.

It was a question of adopting 'tunnel' vision. We had to leave our worries at the gates of

Once we had got our first win it was all systems go. The confidence began to come back, and things just snowballed from there. I had felt confident all along, because we had too many good players to struggle. We just needed a bit of luck to help restore confidence.

In the space of a few weeks, the club was transformed. Players who had been very subdued, and disappointed with themselves, perked up.

Once the team got on the right track, players like Kerry Dixon, Gordon Durie, Kevin Wilson and even Graham Roberts started to score freely.

Personally I've never scored a lot of goals. I really should have worked harder on my finishing over the years, but my responsibilities have always been more on the defensive side.

occasions. Several times we have looked on course to qualify for either the World Cup or the European Championship Finals, only to fail at the last minute.

I've also been disappointed by not winning more honours at club level. When I first started with Crystal Place, we were labelled 'the team of the 80's' when we won the Second Division Championship. But the side was not allowed to develop. Manager Terry Venables left, and the team disintegrated.

I moved on to Arsenal, but there again things didn't really work out for me. There are not many bigger clubs than the Arsenal, but it seems I joined them at the wrong time. The club was going through a mediocre spell, and things didn't improve until my old Palace team-mate George Graham took over as manager, and by then I'd moved on to Luton Town.

I enjoyed my time there despite having to play on the plastic pitch at Kenilworth Road. But when I moved up to Aberdeen, I really felt I was going to experience the best period of my career.

Moving to Scotland gave me the chance to play European club football for the first time.

I was looking forward to years of playing in Europe, and winning domestic honours with Aberdeen, when I discovered the health problems of our new baby.

That meant my career had to change direction again. But I have no regrets now. After all my near misses in the past, I feel I can make up for it with Chelsea.

I believe I'm with a club that can become one of the biggest in Britain – I couldn't ask for more.

PETER NICHOLAS GIVES THE INSIDE STORY ON THE STAMFORD BRIDGE REVIVAL.

Stamford Bridge, and concentrate on football once we got inside.

The players responded. Everybody got on with the task of getting out of the Second Division — although we had to survive a nightmare start to achieve it.

The first month was a total disaster. We didn't win any of our first six matches, and we were bottom of the Second Division.

That was when the character of the players really began to come through. Things could have gone from bad to worse after that start. But they didn't. The players knuckled down.

At Chelsea, Bobby Campbell wants me to play a 'holding' role in midfield, helping out the defence when necessary. And at international level, quite a few of my recent appearances for Wales have been as a defender.

I have just completed ten years of international football with Wales, and hope to carry on for quite a few years yet. When I first played for Wales I was alongside Terry Yorath in midfield. Now he is the manager I aim to continue our association. I'm always proud to pull on the Welsh shirt.

It's very disappointing that in my ten years with Wales we have always just missed out on the big

BILL WILLIAMS isn't the type of player to be found horsing around on the field. He's far too busy shoring up the Stockport County defence for that.

But it's a different story for Bill off the pitch. There, the 28-year-old centre-half can often be found indulging in some real horse play — with his father's fourteen magnificent pedigree Shire horses.

"Dad keeps the horses in fields near where I live, so it's no bother for me to lend a hand," says Bill. "My father employs a full-time helper and has my brother Peter mucking in, but there is still a lot of work for me to do.

"For a start the horses all need feeding, six-thirty every morning on the dot. They're a hungry lot though, and one meal a day just won't do. It's the same time every evening as well, and that's usually where I come in," explains Bill.

"My dad took up the hobby about six years ago. Originally he and a friend had the idea of setting up a dray, a horse and cart similar to those used by breweries, to display at shows. Unfortunately that brainchild fell through and he decided to go ahead with the Shires alone.

"Then a couple of years ago he took a step into breeding — hence his current total of fourteen pedigree horses. If you want to make money then this is where it lies," Bill goes on. "Normal run-of-the-mill Shires fetch about £5,000. Pedigree stallions on the other hand are more likely to cost roughly four times as much.

"Naturally the horses don't just stand in their fields all week looking nice. Like footballers they have very busy weekends — on show. My dad has a large horse-box which he uses when going to shows up and down the country. He's away somewhere or other almost every weekend.

HORSE PLAY!

That's just the job for Stockport County's BILL WILLIAMS.

"Over the years my father has even become a regular at Wembley — every footballer's dream. I'm not too envious though. It's the Horse of the Year Show at the Wembley Arena where he performs.

"His two major prize-winners are Royal, who has a total of twelve championships to his name, and Rosy. She was his latest Wembley entrant and doesn't get around as often as the others, hence only six championship wins. However, she has been judged the eighth finest horse in Britain so I expect that counts for something as well," says Bill.

"I think that now he has fourteen horses my father won't be adding to that. He'll keep breeding for other people but has his hands full with our little lot.

"As for me, I'm quite happy watching the odd show with the family and lending an occasional hand. I certainly don't think I'll be buying any stock of my own. I know just how hard a life it can be," ends Bill.

Aston Villa's **ALAN McINALLY** is in the thick of things as he spearheads a raid on the Millwall goal.

LAST season was the best-ever for Norwich City and for me personally. I hope we can both go on to better things in the future. Yet few people know how close I was to missing it all, perhaps drifting out of top class football altogether.

The previous season I was out of the side at Norwich, and going nowhere. Certainly my career was not progressing. I was out of condition, and my attitude was all wrong.

I knew I had to do something about it. I was at a cross-roads in my career. That was when my girl-friend Lisa, now my wife, took a hand. Once I'd made my mind up to work at things, she took control of my diet.

During that close season she kept me on a strict diet of just 1000 calories a day. If I went over the limit, she let me know I was out of order!

In about three weeks I lost a stone in weight. I went on six-mile training runs each day during the close season, so that by the time I went back for pre-season training I had a head-start on the other players.

All the dieting and training made me feel great. At the start of last season I was raring to go, determined to regain the form that had earned me my League debut at the age of 17. Things just went from there. The team started the season well, and we maintained our form right through the campaign.

I believe my extra fitness was reflected in my performances. I was able to work hard for the full 90 minutes. Instead of flashing in and out of matches, as in the past, I could work up and down the right side covering back in defence, and still making runs when we had the ball.

Now I've got my mind on the job, I never want to go back to my old ways. I'm determined to make the most of my ability.

I was married to Lisa this summer. But months before our honeymoon I had worked out tough training schedules to follow in the second week of our holiday, so that I would report back to Carrow Road in good shape.

I feel I have grown up about three years in the space of a few months. I've set myself standards in the last year that I'm determined to maintain. One very good season is not enough. The best players carry it on for year after year, and that is now my target.

A few years ago I was in the same England Boy and Youth teams as Arsenal players Tony Adams, David Rocastle and Michael Thomas. They all progressed to the England senior squad, while I marked time. Now I want to catch them up again.

I'm known as 'Flash' at Carrow Road. But not because I'm flashy. My nickname comes from the old film star Flash Gordon. It's an improvement on the first nickname I was saddled with at Norwich, one which gave me the wrong image altogether.

That was 'Disco', but I was not out every night disco dancing as people seemed to think. But as a youngster I did enjoy going dancing. So our physio Tim Sheppard gave me the nickname Disco.

It looked bad for me. It seemed as if I spent all my time in discos. So I was glad to get rid of the name. I want to be recognised as a footballer, not a disco dancer.

It's amazing that I'm the longest serving player at Carrow Road — at the age of 22. I made my debut at the age of 17, and none of the other players in that side is still with the club.

I played several matches in the build-up to Norwich's Milk Cup Final against Sunderland four years

ago, but didn't get a place at Wembley, which was a let-down.

I think it's always tough to establish yourself in the side as a local lad. You're always under more pressure than players who come from other areas.

It can be difficult for a young player to be consistent, particularly a forward who is trying to do things with the ball. That's why I was so pleased with my consistency last season. We've got a team at Norwich that doesn't have any superstars. We just plug away, working for each other as a unit.

In the past, Norwich always had a reputation for not travelling well. Our away record used to be poor. But last season we won more games away than we did at home, and it was all down to our hard-working approach.

A few times I saw statements like 'stop Dale Gordon and you stop Norwich' or 'when Dale Gordon plays well, Norwich play well'. But I take no notice of things like that, except as a compliment and a boost to my confidence.

I don't see myself as any better than anyone else in the Norwich side, but it is nice to feel that other people are recognising me as a force in the game.

All I want to do is make sure that I don't get carried away by our success last season. My aim is to keep my feet firmly on the ground. I've been up there before, and fallen flat on my face, and I'm determined not to let that happen again.

I still enjoy a laugh and joke with the lads, but I gear my whole approach to each match. I very rarely go out of an evening, especially not within three days of a match.

Last season after our F.A. Cup quarter-final against West Ham, when we won through after a Wednesday night replay, a mate asked me to go out to celebrate getting through to the semi-final. I

HARD WORK HAS PAID

elected to go home and get my head down, because we had a League match on the Saturday. That sums up my new dedication to the game. I think I am being professional in my approach.

It would be great if all the hard work I've put in for the last year and a half would pay off with a place in the England squad.

At Norwich I feel we don't get the recognition we would receive if we were in London or one of the big cities. Players with the 'big five' — Arsenal, Spurs, Manchester United, Liverpool and Everton — get much more exposure from the live television matches, and media coverage.

In Norwich people are a bit quiet, and don't push themselves very much. Our manager, Dave Stringer, doesn't speak out a lot, he just gets on with the job. Nobody has really given him any attention but he's done a great job for the club.

I would love to pull on an England shirt again. It would be a tremendous reward for all my hard work. But at the moment I am concentrating all my efforts on maintaining my form at club level.

An international cap would be the cream on the cake. But League football is the bread and butter — and that comes first.

That's the proud claim of Norwich City's DALE GORDON.

OFF!

DAVID SMITH
Coventry

CHARLIE
NICHOLAS
Aberdeen

TAKE OFF!

Arsenal's STEVE BOULD hits the heights as he brushes aside the challenge of Everton's TONY COTTEE.

PAT NEVIN *Everton*

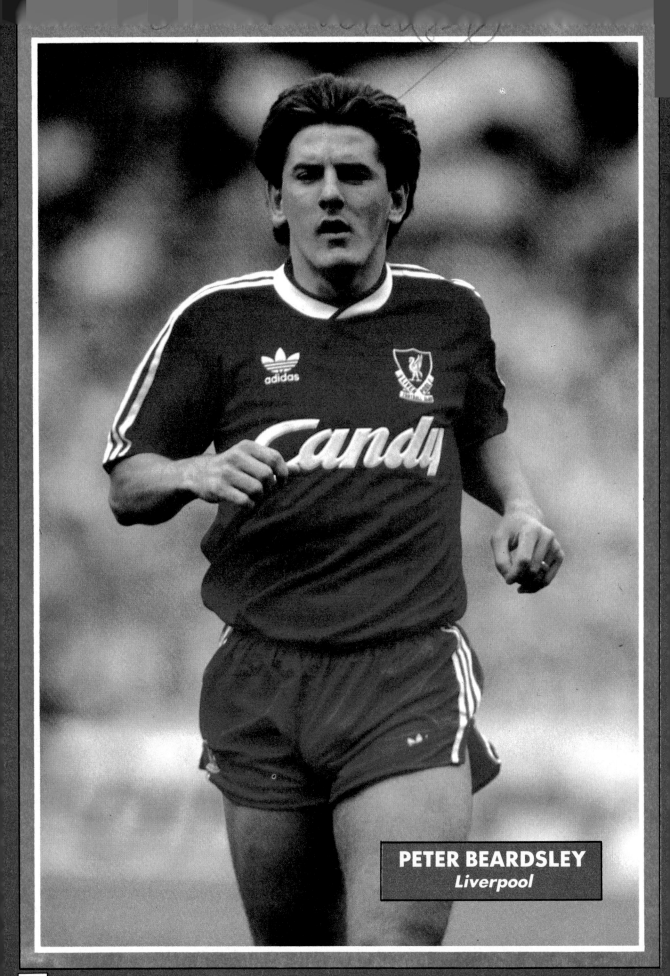

PETER BEARDSLEY
Liverpool

STUART GRAY *Aston Villa*

TERRY FENWICK

I COMPLETED an unusual 'hat-trick' when I signed for Spurs nearly two years ago. For the third time in my career I was putting pen to paper for manager Terry Venables.

He has been the major influence on my career. Most of what I've achieved in football is down to him — my England caps, two Second Division Championship medals, and an F.A. Cup runners'-up medal.

In fact I've got only one regret in football — and that is that I couldn't persuade Terry to sign me on one other occasion! That was after the boss had left Queen's Park Rangers, having taken us to fifth place in the First Division in the season immediately after winning promotion.

Terry went to take over at Barcelona, one of the most famous clubs in the world. I'd always wanted to play for a really big team. And having been one of his first signings for Rangers, from Palace, I hoped he would take me to Spain as well.

But no such luck! Terry needed strikers such as Steve Archibald, Mark Hughes and Gary Lineker at Barcelona, not a defender like myself.

However, once he had returned to England, to take over at Tottenham, he made me his first signing for Spurs. Tottenham is perhaps not as big as Barcelona, but you can't get much bigger, and better, than Spurs in Britain.

When Terry asked me to join him at Tottenham, the side was struggling in the lower half of the table. Things

SPURS' TERRY FENWICK TALKS
INFLUENCE OF MANAGER TERRY

IT'S TE
AND TER
AGA

were not going too well. At the same time, George Graham, manager of Arsenal, who were near the top of the table, approached me to join the Gunners.

What a predicament! Two fantastic clubs, managed by men I really respected, both wanting me. It's the kind of problem anybody would love to have.

I knew George Graham from his time as coach at Crystal Palace. I had enormous respect for him. But when I knew that Terry Venables wanted me, my mind was made up for me. The fact that Spurs were struggling, while Arsenal were in the running for honours, never came into it.

Terry has something extra special as a manager. He's proved that to me time and time again over the last ten years.

What makes him so outstanding is his handling of players and his approach to the game. Because he was such a good player himself — and a very talented one, at that — he can appreciate the problems of players. He understands what they are thinking and what their moods are.

Terry can get the best out of individuals because he knows how their minds work. He's not afraid to give talented players the chance to express themselves on the pitch.

I joined Crystal Palace as a youngster when Terry was coach to Malcolm Allison. I thought the world of Malcolm as a manager, and it was very apparent he had a very high regard for Terry.

It wasn't long before Terry took over as manager, and led the side into the First Division by giving youngsters their chance.

Kenny Sansom, Peter Nicholas, Billy Gilbert, Jerry Murphy, Vince Hilaire and myself all established ourselves in the Palace side as teenagers at around the same time.

We have all had good careers in the game — and I wonder what might have happened if we had all stayed at Selhurst Park. But Terry quit not long after getting us into the First Division, and after he went, the side broke up.

Together with Mike Flanagan, I was Terry's first signing for Queen's Park Rangers. At the time, Rangers were fourth from the bottom of Division Two, while Palace were still in the First. But Terry had impressed me so much that I had no hesitation in joining him at Loftus Road.

By the end of that first season we had zoomed up the table, thanks to a run of 12 wins in 13 games. We just missed out on promotion. The following season we got to the F.A. Cup Final before losing to Spurs in a replay. That's still one of the highlights of my career — in particular scoring the equaliser in the dying minutes of the first match.

A year later we won the Second Division, and followed up with fifth place in the First the next season. It was progress all the time, on and off the field, at Rangers.

I believe it was basically

all down to the manager's ideas. He had a great Chairman in Jim Gregory, who backed him with money to develop the club, but it was Terry's willingness to try new things and always look ahead that started it all.

I was still a young lad in football terms when I went to Rangers. I didn't always appreciate at the time what Terry was doing.

For instance he'd put things on in training — different drills or tactical routines, or set pieces — and for no apparent reason. But about three or four games later it would hit you what it was all about.

Terry always worked two, three, four games ahead of everybody else. You'd suddenly meet situations in matches that we had worked on in training a week or two before. It all fell into place afterwards.

It was a big loss to Rangers when Terry left to join Barcelona. The players missed him, and I think the Chairman missed him even more.

My first year and a half at Spurs wasn't easy. But never once did I regret joining, or wish that I'd opted for Arsenal instead.

I was confident all along that Terry would get things right in the end. And the final two or three months of last season produced signs that he had got the blend and the balance right.

For over a year at White Hart Lane, Terry had to put up with a bashing from the press and television. Everybody was knocking him

and the team because he'd spent a lot of money, and results were not good.

But one of Terry's strong points is that criticism just bounces off him. He didn't react at all. Just let us get on with our job, and let the papers print what they wanted.

He carried on experimenting with the players he had, buying, selling, trying new ideas. We used a sweeper system for some of the time. Tried different formations with three, four, sometimes five players in midfield.

He gave several young players the chance to show what they could do. Switched others around, myself included, to find where they were most effective.

I played as a sweeper, as a central defender, in midfield, and at full-back last season. Ideally I would prefer to settle into one place. But for a manager like Terry Venables I will play anywhere, as long as I'm in the team.

A few years ago I wanted to settle down in the centre of defence. I felt it was my best chance of gaining an international place with England.

Nowadays I think my international days are past, and I'm happy to let the younger players fight for the places in the England side. After the European Championship failure I felt Bobby Robson had to put his faith in younger blood — people like Paul Gascoigne, for example.

Paul has fantastic talent, and it's just a matter of getting the best out of him. Last season was a bit up-and-down for him. He had to overcome all the problems associated with being a £2.2 million player. I feel that in the next year he will be superb. He can become the man around whom the England side can be shaped in the future.

I would never give up hope of getting a new call-up to the England squad. But when I see all the top youngsters around, I'm happy to have played the matches I did for England.

Playing in the World Cup in Mexico was an experience I'll never forget — even if it ended so disappointingly. Maradona 'conned' the referee for the goal he punched past Peter Shilton, and then he turned on the skill to leave me and half the side trailing, as he scored the second goal that beat us in the quarter-final.

Not even Terry Venables could have taught me to cope with that!

RRY RY— IN!

TERRY VENABLES

RIVALS!

Tottenham Hotspur's **PAUL WALSH** (left) tangles with **MARK REID** (Charlton) as the London rivals do battle.

PAUL LAKE *Manchester City*

NO REST FOR RODGER!

TEN years ago, disillusionment with newspaper football coverage, set Rodger Wylde to preparing for a career after his playing days. The one-time Sheffield Wednesday, Oldham Athletic, Sunderland, Barnsley and Stockport County striker went to college to study shorthand, typing and word processing.

It was Rodger's first step towards becoming a football reporter.

"I kept reading reports of matches I'd played in and thinking, 'that didn't happen'. For example," Rodger explains, "I would be credited as having scored with a volley when in fact it was a header. Eventually there came a point when I thought I could do better than the journalists.

"So I enrolled for the college course after having a word with a friend of mine on a local paper in Sheffield. My next step was to go to matches with experienced newspapermen to observe how they went about their job.

"Then, about four years ago, I had my first real taste of journalism. I began doing the occasional match report for the Sheffield Saturday evening sports paper 'The Green 'Un!'

"It was then that I realised how mistakes are made. When I actually began to report on games, I noticed how hard it was to properly identify players on the pitch or to get incidents down in the right order. It isn't as easy as some people think!

"But my work with The Green 'Un couldn't really last because I was still playing at the time."

But that wasn't to mean an end to the goal-getter's newspaper career. It was restarted just about eighteen months ago thanks to another local Sheffield publication 'The South Yorkshire Times.'

"A full-time vacancy came up in the sports department of the paper," Rodger recounts. "But although full-time wasn't entirely suitable for me, I was contracted to write my own weekly column.

"During the football season I concentrate on interviews with

TIMES SPORT

TOUGH GUY TONY'S SOCCER SHOCKER!

Rodger Wylde

From being shot at on foreign soil defending the oil arteries of the Middle east, to writing books and living the life of a well paid fitness expert, Tony Toms, the former assistant manager of Sheffield Wednesday, gave evidence which explained his cruelly cynical, carefree outlook on life.

"Initially," answered Tony quite seriously, talking about the transition from Marines to pro soccer. "I was shocked, from being surrounded by real men in the commandos to having the company of men who were like a load of brownies by comparison."

He thought for a moment than altered his claim, "No, that's not fair, probably girl guides is a better description..."

His profound and undoubtable confidence was shaped from the day he enlisted in the elite commando regiment in 1959, of strength and endurance that only those of undeniable material can emerge. As Tony explains. "The Marines is a very hard life, but if you can take all the training in your stride and come out at the other end intact and it can also be a very rewarding career".

After reaching the top rank in his chosen field

One of the T.V. programmes was to feature Tony training a football team over a period ... Hartlepool United. "I'd never heard of the place", smiled Tony. "It might as well have been in Bolivia for all I knew. Anyway, I went up there, trained the team and from previously gaining eleven points from 28 games they won their next eight matches. Len Ashurst, then manager of Hartlepool and, he adds with typical forces wit "a right pain in the bum", offered me some money which compared to marine pay seemed like a fortune. I accepted and became assistant manager of a team playing a game I knew absolutely nothing about."

The pair elevated Hartlepool to practically the summit of the Fourth Division before Gillingham ambushed them and here they performed the miracle of resurecting them into the Third Division. At this time, in 1975, the Wednesday job was vacant and being an ambitious duo they applied for and got the job. But as Tony bluntly admitted, "At Hillsborough we inherited the worst set of players we had ever come across did well without having money to sp balanced the books financiall

Moors on a cold winter's night to spend the dark hours exposed to the elements with only a sleeping bag for protection. After this excursion the team won their next eight games!

During his years with the Marines was there a time when he was in a volatile situation? "Hell, I'll say there was. I used to love the bang, bang of the blank shells on the firing range," narrates Tony. "There I thought I was real hero. Then one day we were shipped out to Radfan on the Yemen border to defend the oil pipelines from the Arabs. I can tell you that when those bullets are for real and aimed at you to kill, I was turned inside out and realised I was no hero."

Tony, whose hobbies include water skiing, now owns a weight training and Body Building gym in Sheffield.

So what did he not enjoy about soccer? "The game was great. It was just the people in it - they bored the pants off me," was his blatant reply.

By the way, if you ever go into Tomsy's gym for a work out, you will recognise him straight away - he's the one that's built like the proverbial brick outside toilet.

the European

I NEED TO DO WELL AT WEDNESDAY – HODGSON

Rodger Wylde

David Hodgson must see this opportunity with Sheffield Wednesday in the First Division as his last chance to establish himself in top class football and also as a break on a rapidly declining career that had plummeted since leaving one of England's premier clubs.

The former Middlesborough and Liverpool striker has disappointed at a number of clubs since leaving Anfield in 1984, costing Sunderland £250,000 where, during the Laurie McMenemy regime, he was kept in the reserves, because, as David says in his mild Geordie accent, "McMenemy told me I didn't score enough goals for a striker, even though Sunderland at the time were struggling at the bottom of the league and I had knocked in 27 goals in the reserves. He said I could do as good a job as the lads already playing.

"My natural game is to work across the line making runs, creating chances for others, this is what I did for Middlesbrough and Liverpool. Although I remember a few games into one particular season I was leading scorer with seven goals and Ian Rush hadn't got off the mark."

Then he adds with a grin. "But by the end of

Norwich City. On his debut for the Canaries he scored a sizzling hat-trick, but in subsequent games failed to find the net again - so once again he found himself a free agent at the end of the season.

This rapid decline from commanding quarter of a million pounds price tags to suddenly finding himself in football's bargain basement didn't affect David's confidence. "I knew that I hadn't become a bad player overnight. I had got personal problems, plus I was two stone overweight, which took its toll on my performances."

Last year, like so many English players before him, David took the sunny Pesata of Cadiz of Spain where he hoped to resurect his flagging career. Again fate seemed to be twisting his arm up his back as the fat contract he signed dried up financially after a few months in Spain leaving him penniless with the police banging on his door arrest him for non-payment of a car-hire he situation had been explained sympath

experienced the peaks and troughs of a football life.

At the beginning of August newly promoted Cardiff City manager Frank Burrows offered David a career lifeline in Third Division. Terms were agreed over the phone and the contract was to be signed at Ninian Park the following day. Due to a delayed train David arrived to later sign that evening, as he explains, "The late train meant that the contract was to be finalised the next day, so Frank took me to a hotel to stay overnight - while I was in my room Peter Eustace phoned expressing Wednesday's interest, but because Frank Burrows had been so good to me I said that the only way I would sign for Wednesday was if their terms were better than Cardiff's and the offer was a definite one.

"Early the next morning Howard Wilkinson rang me, made me an offer and said that the two year contract was waiting to be signed in Sheffield."

Now David is hoping the move to Wednesday will revive his flagging career - as in the case of ex-Owl Lee Chapman?

"I would love to do half as well as Lee did in his time at Hillsboro
player and I

---

footballers from our local clubs — Sheffield Wednesday, Sheffield United, Barnsley, Rotherham United and Doncaster Rovers.

"In the close season, however, the column takes on a somewhat different slant. I invite readers to throw me any kind of challenge," Rodger continues.

"A couple of summers ago, for example, I was asked by the Rotherham Redskins American Football team to give their sport a go.

"The experience was frightening! I played as a quarter-back and soon had the bruises to prove it. I did manage to get the ball away to one of my side a couple of times, but more often than not I was throwing it anywhere to avoid being flattened by onrushing giants.

"I was also asked to try my hand at windsurfing, something else I hadn't done before. I really enjoyed my day on the water and because of it have taken up the sport myself. It's great fun. Who knows what I'll be asked to do in the future?"

What Rodger may be asked to do is join one of the national daily papers. This idea, though, is one the much-travelled striker is not keen on.

"It's not really my ambition to join one of the nationals. That doesn't really interest me. I would much rather get out and about meeting and talking to people. After close on 20 years as a footballer I just couldn't be stuck in an office all week."

During all those years in the game, Rodger has worked hard to make sure he had a future when his playing days were over.

"Football is a very insecure profession, and with that in mind I set about making sure I was well prepared for a career after it. I have sat O-Levels, management courses, shorthand and typing and

picked up a bit of Portuguese during my time with Sporting Lisbon.

"A lot of time, though, has gone into qualifying as a physiotherapist. I finally achieved that last summer. I have my own treatment centre just about to be completed near Sheffield. Hopefully I'll set up business there.

"It has a clinic and a full gymnasium but it isn't the kind of gym for body-building courses or the like. I intend the treatment to be on a one to one basis, or at most one to two. This way it is

more personal and patients may respond better.

"Once that is off the ground and I'm combining it with my work for the paper, my next intention is to learn a lauguage. I learnt a little Portuguese in Lisbon but would like to have a go at another one," closes Rodger.

Whatever next? Rodger Wylde — Foreign Correspondent?

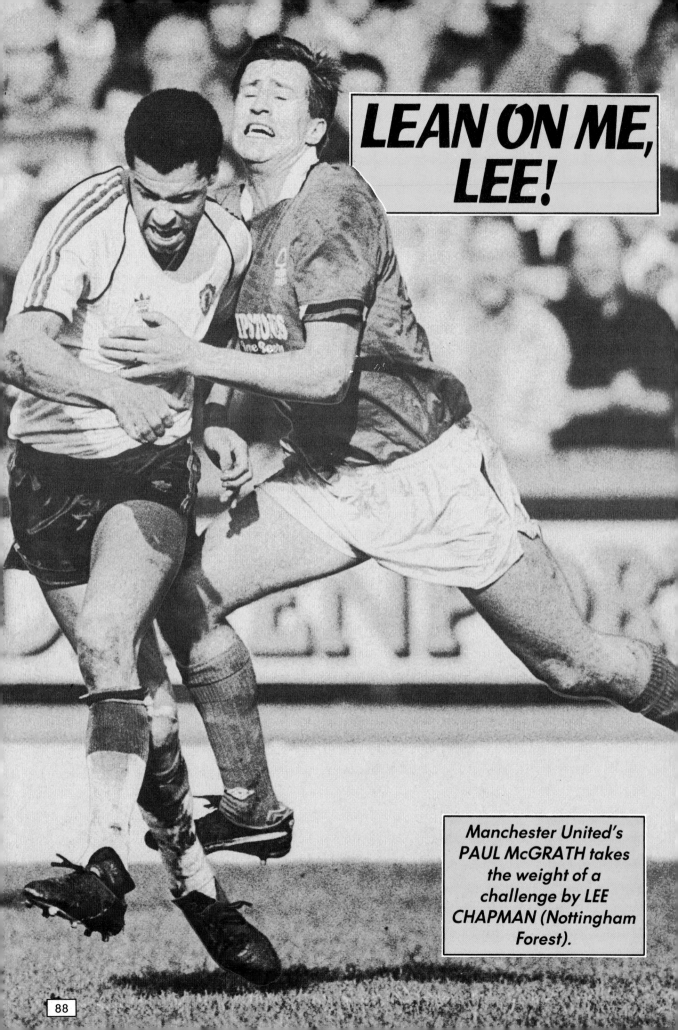

LEAN ON ME, LEE!

Manchester United's **PAUL McGRATH** takes the weight of a challenge by **LEE CHAPMAN** (Nottingham Forest).

NIGEL WINTERBURN *Arsenal*

GOOD START – SHAME ABOUT THE FINISH!

THE verdict on my own performance last season was identical to that which I would have delivered on my club, Aston Villa.

It read, 'Started well, and promised great things. Slumped in mid-season and finished on a disappointing note.

'Must regard the campaign as a successful settling-in process during first year back. But should learn lessons, build on those and put on a much better showing in the future.'

It's no surprise that my own report should coincide with that of the whole side — because even as we approached last season we were running on parallel courses.

After three years of Italian football, I was returning to my previous club to make a First Division comeback. It was very much a case of hoping that I could settle back quickly.

Similarly, Villa themselves were returning to the top flight after a year's absence, having just won promotion from the Second. In the end, I have to say that the season was a rather frustrating one.

Personally, I was pleased with the way I played during the first half of the campaign. After Christmas, however, I lost form, and, just as I felt it was returning, I suffered a torn medial ligament in my knee. By the time I recovered, the season was virtually over.

As far as the team was concerned, we also started well, but fell away during the second half of the season and eventually found ourselves battling against relegation. In the end, we survived and there was a lot of consolation in that.

For one thing, we'd retained our newly-won place among the top clubs. For another, several of the players at Villa Park were making their First Division debuts.

That meant coming up against the best in the League for the first time and making their initial appearances at some of the country's top stadiums. That experience must stand them in good stead for the future.

For my own future, I have to take a few more positive steps towards reaching the same level that I'd attained before I went to Italy.

I was a regular midfield player with one of the top clubs in the country. And, before breaking a leg two years earlier, I had started to earn a regular slot in Bobby Robson's international side.

In the end, two of my three years in Italy were a complete waste of time. Yet, when I joined Bari in the summer of 1985, everything went well for the first year. I felt as fit as ever, my form had returned and I

GRAHAM TAYLOR

was enjoying my football. I was playing in the Italian First Division and facing big-name clubs every week.

The big change came at the end of that first season, however. We were relegated, and suddenly my continental dream turned sour.

For the next two years, I felt I was being buried in the obscurity of Second Division football. I honestly believed that I was good enough to play at a higher level.

It hurt me that people back home were also forgetting all about me. If I'd been playing in the same division as clubs such as

Juventus and AC Milan the English fans would still have had regular reports about how I was getting on.

As it was, having stepped down a division, that coverage stopped. No news of my progress filtered through at all.

Consequently, I spent virtually two years trying to get back to England. At one stage Jim Smith, who was then manager of Queen's Park Rangers, tried to take me to Loftus Road.

But Bari refused to do business — even though I begged the club president to let me return.

I told him that I wasn't enjoying my football and, because that was the only reason I'd come to Italy in the first place, it was making my whole life miserable.

He refused, reasoning that he couldn't consider selling the club's top players at a time when they were going all out to win promotion back to the First Division.

In the end, it took the finish of my contract with the club to pave the way for my return to Villa.

There was just one problem. I knew the Villa fans would be expecting to see the same player who had starred in the side which won the League Championship and European Cup in the early 1980's.

Having spoken to manager Graham Taylor around Christmas, I'd voiced my doubts to him. I didn't believe then that rejoining my old club would be a good move. I couldn't be sure I'd be able to live up to the fans' expectations, and felt it might be better to make my Football League comeback with a different club.

But Graham wasn't put off, and when we had further talks, he convinced me that Villa was the right club.

The more I thought about it, the more I realised how happy my family would be to return to their old surroundings in the Midlands. When the move was made, I experienced a tremendous feeling of relief.

Having said that, I never

regretted going to Italy. In spite of those two miserable years, my spell in the Italian League helped my game.

The style of play is much slower there. Defences are much more difficult to break down. Not because their defenders are more skilful, but because they defend in such great numbers.

It means you have to think more, rather that just play by instinct. As a midfield player, I found that prospect very challenging.

I also had to come to terms with the Italians' fear of losing possession. On many occasions I saw the possibility of attacking on the break — situations which screamed for a long ball from defence into attack.

The Italians, however, are so frightened of giving the ball away, nothing will make them take such a

of the action just passed me by, and it was quite a shock to be reminded that you just don't have time to dwell on the ball in English football.

So I knew that my settling-in wasn't going to be complete in just a few weeks. I had to gradually accustom myself to the tempo of the English First Division.

But I didn't want any ready-made excuses if I went through periods of poor form. I made my comeback convinced that I was as ready as I'd ever be. And I was also sure that I was capable of playing as well, if not better than I did during my first spell with Villa.

With one full season under my belt since returning, I've begun the task of doing that. This season I am fully determined to improve even further.

There is still some way to go, of

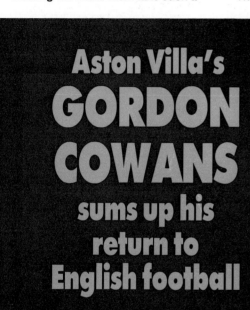

Aston Villa's
GORDON COWANS
sums up his return to English football

risk. They just keep on building slowly until they are in the last third of the field. I found that very frustrating. But, at the same time, it added something new to my game.

My first touch improved. That gained me a few seconds and an extra yard of space in which to make better use of the ball. My brain became sharper as a result of competing with the wiles of the Italian game.

All told, I came back to England a better player than when I departed. That was something I was keen to prove when I stepped back on the English stage — but I knew it would take time to do so.

For example, my first game back was against Millwall, and those 90 minutes made me realise just how much of an adjustment I would have to make.

The pace was incredible. Most

course. For example, I've not come close to England recognition again.

But that's something I can still aim for in the future. All I can do is play the best I can and hope that the recognition will come again. But that's something I can still aim for in the future. All I can do is play the best I can and hope that I can force my way back into contention again for a place in the England squad.

MARK HUGHES *Manchester Utd.*

BALL WATCHERS!

Derby County's PAUL GODDARD (left) and BRIAN KILCLINE (Coventry) both set their sights on winning possession of that ball.

93

MANCHESTER CITY'S
NEIL McNAB
RELISHES LIFE IN THE FIRST DIVISION

I'M a First Division player again after securing promotion from the Second for the third time in my career. I'm back in the top flight at the age of 32 and I don't envisage any problems in making that step up.

I reckon I've always played my best football in Division One. I was at my peak at 28-29 the last time Manchester City were in the First. Was in good form, too, when my previous clubs — Brighton, Bolton and Spurs — were 'upstairs'.

I love playing against big name international players. I rise to the occasion. And I enjoy the extra time and space you are given at that level. Not that I believe I've played badly in the Second in recent years. Far from it. I've been very pleased with my contribution at Maine Road.

I've been very much the old hand of the side. That's a label which is bound to stick when you're ten years senior to many of your team-mates. And at City these past few seasons, we've fielded a lot of young players.

I've enjoyed helping them along. I've always been a talker on the field and I've probably done more just recently. Giving encouragement is the main thing. It doesn't help youngsters' development if you criticise too much.

At Maine Road we had five players called into the England Under-21 squad last season. Steve Redmond, David White, Andy Hinchcliffe, Paul Lake and Ian Brightwell are high quality players and will have

big futures in the game.

I was delighted to see them develop the way they did. One day I hope to be sitting at Wembley watching some of them play for the full England side. They all have the ability and I have to admit the youngsters have helped my game, too. They are exciting to play with.

It's the presence of that batch of young players which makes me believe City have a brighter First Division future than when we were promoted four years ago. Then we lasted just two seasons at top level before being relegated again.

These lads are definitely First Division players. Survival won't be a problem. The biggest difficulty is always getting there.

The Second is a very hard

division. There are a lot of good sides in it. I'm sure we will have easier matches in the First than we had last season.

There's no question in my mind that this is a better City team than the last one to win promotion. I feel it could be in the First for years.

The side reminds me of Brian Clough's Nottingham Forest team. He has a young team at the City Ground which has been very successful. I expect the lads here to become every bit as good.

It will take time. Forest are better than us and are probably a year ahead in their development. They have come on by leaps and bounds in the past year or so. I'm hoping our young players will develop at a similar rate.

But it isn't just a batch of

youngsters and myself at Maine Road. We have a core of experienced pros in their mid-twenties. And they seem to get forgotten sometimes amid all the praise the kids come in for.

Outstanding last season, for instance, was goalkeeper Andy Dibble. I would place him amongst the top three 'keepers in the League. He's just unlucky to be on form at the same time as Neville Southall or he would have won a sackful of caps for Wales.

There were stages last term when he was playing so well I just couldn't see opposing sides scoring against him. He is the best goalie I've played in front of since I was in the same side as Pat Jennings during my early days at Spurs.

For my own part last season, I know I played pretty

well. Certainly I did more towards my third promotion success than I did towards my second.

My first was at White Hart Lane back in 1978. I played a full League season for Spurs that year. I was coming up to 21 years of age. The sort of age the City youngsters are now.

The next time was in 1985. By then I'd moved to Maine Road. But during that season I started only 15 matches and I was struggling with my form.

During the following years, however, as I've become the senior player, I've taken on more responsibility, and my form has kept on improving.

I play a different game these days as well. In my younger days I dribbled too much. Now I tend to let the ball do the work. My job is to start things from deep positions. I like being involved the whole time.

During the four years between the City promotions, I've seen an awful lot of players come and go.

I knew that having been here six years I was the club's longest-serving player. But until I started totting them all up, I didn't realise just how many had been used.

For instance, 14 players were bought during that last promotion campaign and over the next couple of years when we were trying to stay in the First. Amazingly, none of them is still with the club.

Those signings were good players and the team was strengthened sufficiently to take us up. But it probably wasn't a side built with the long-term in mind.

The approach has been different this time. Manager Mel Machin has built around youth. Mel's particular strength is working with young players. He'll see to it we become an even better team.

I've watched these kids go into action under his management and they are not afraid to make mistakes. That's a very important factor in the development of young talent.

When you know your manager has confidence in your ability the chances are you'll be able to take the knocks that are all part and parcel of a footballer's life.

BERNIE SLAVEN *Middlesbrough*

Second Time Lucky

for Bristol Rovers 'keeper NIGEL MARTYN.

My big break in football came in most unusual circumstances. I come from a part of the world that produces far more rugby players than footballers. That's my home county of Cornwall.

Perhaps the most famous Cornish footballer was Mike Trebilcock who scored two goals in the 1966 F.A. Cup Final to help Everton to a dramatic victory over Sheffield Wednesday. That happened three months before I was born.

Mike Trebilcock put Cornwall on the football map but I'd like to go one better by actually playing for England one day. I've taken the first steps towards realising that ambition by playing for the Under-21's.

But playing for England at all would have been just a dream while I was still living in Cornwall. Even League football seemed fairly remote in a county that doesn't have a single team in any of the four divisions.

The top level football in Cornwall is the South-Western League. I played for a local team, St. Blazey, and I couldn't really see myself moving on from there.

The standard wasn't too bad but it was a long way from League football. Who was going to notice a young goalkeeper playing for a team like St. Blazey?

So I was taken by surprise when Plymouth Argyle asked me to go for a trial. They were the nearest big club, across the border in Devon.

I hadn't expected to get that sort of opportunity but I decided I should try to make the most of it. But in the event, I never had that chance.

On the day of the trial it poured with rain. Plymouth decided to call off the trial. I thought they would arrange a new date but I never heard from them again. I thought that was that, so I returned to my job in St. Austell.

Later on I went to work in a local plastics factory and it was soon after that I was given a surprising second chance by a League club. It wasn't Plymouth this time, but Bristol Rovers.

· I had a local fan to thank for the opportunity. He was a chap from a local carpet shop who had watched me play for St. Blazey. I suppose he must have been quite impressed by what he saw because he rang up Rovers boss

Gerry Francis to point him in my direction.

Gerry then invited me up for a practice match and this time it did actually take place. That was just as well for me because Gerry was impressed enough by what he saw to offer me a contract. It meant a complete change of lifestyle for me but I didn't hesitate for long.

Bristol Rovers aren't one of the biggest clubs in the League and they don't even play at their own ground, but it was still a different world for me.

One thing that wasn't different from Cornwall was the interest in rugby in the area, especially in Bath where we play our home games. But thankfully there were still quite a few people interested in the fortunes of Bristol Rovers.

I had been expecting to wait quite a while before I got my chance in the first team. I had a lot to learn about being a goalkeeper at this level. But Gerry Francis had other ideas. He put me straight in the team to see what I could do.

I suppose it could have ended disastrously but thankfully it couldn't have gone much better. It didn't seem to be any time at all before Dave Sexton was calling me in to the England Under-21 squad as an over-age player.

I thought I would just get the one game so that he could take a look at me but I managed to play throughout last season. It was very good experience for me.

I was mixing with players from the First Division, which I know is an important part of my education. Even more interesting for me was the opportunity to train with a specialist goalkeeping coach for the first time.

At Bristol Rovers, the club physio was in charge of keeping an eye on me but I was basically teaching myself. Under Mike Kelly with England I was getting my first real coaching. It has helped my game tremendously.

I felt very proud to be representing the Third Division last season along with Wolves' hot-shot striker Steve Bull. I don't think we did too badly between us. Perhaps one day we'll be teaming up again for the full England team.

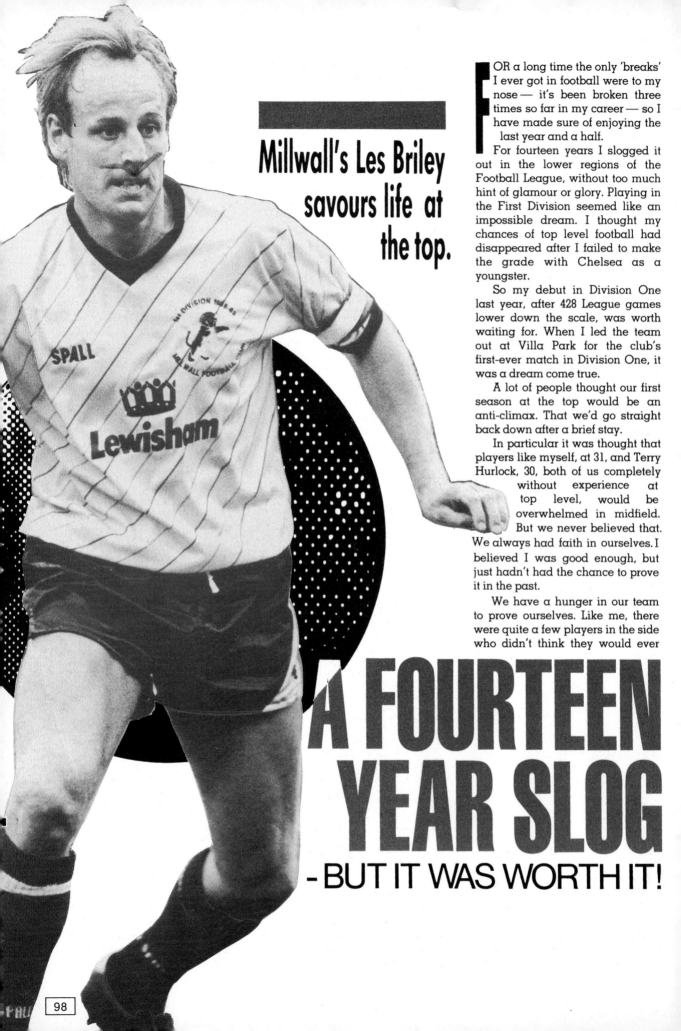

Millwall's Les Briley savours life at the top.

FOR a long time the only 'breaks' I ever got in football were to my nose — it's been broken three times so far in my career — so I have made sure of enjoying the last year and a half.

For fourteen years I slogged it out in the lower regions of the Football League, without too much hint of glamour or glory. Playing in the First Division seemed like an impossible dream. I thought my chances of top level football had disappeared after I failed to make the grade with Chelsea as a youngster.

So my debut in Division One last year, after 428 League games lower down the scale, was worth waiting for. When I led the team out at Villa Park for the club's first-ever match in Division One, it was a dream come true.

A lot of people thought our first season at the top would be an anti-climax. That we'd go straight back down after a brief stay.

In particular it was thought that players like myself, at 31, and Terry Hurlock, 30, both of us completely without experience at top level, would be overwhelmed in midfield. But we never believed that. We always had faith in ourselves. I believed I was good enough, but just hadn't had the chance to prove it in the past.

We have a hunger in our team to prove ourselves. Like me, there were quite a few players in the side who didn't think they would ever

A FOURTEEN YEAR SLOG
– BUT IT WAS WORTH IT!

get the chance to play in the top flight. Players like us have always had to work hard for things, and we didn't stop just because we got into the First Division.

We loved every minute of it last season. I think we surprised a lot of people. But nobody does any dreaming at the Den. It may sound boring, but we think about only the next game. We never look too far ahead. I think that's helped us to keep our feet on the ground.

We work hard and play as a team. We may not be as talented as some outfits, but we are a good unit. The boss, John Docherty kept the same side together that won promotion. He gave us all the chance to play at the top, so the spirit was tremendous.

I just had one regret about our first season. The goal that got away. It was against Arsenal at Highbury. The ball came to me just right and I hit a scorcher from 25 yards that flew past John Lukic into the roof of the net.

It would have been one of the best goals of my life — but the referee ruled it out. I just couldn't believe it. Nobody was interfering with play. I still can't understand how offside could have been given.

The decision was particularly disappointing, because that 'goal' could have won us the match, and we deserved a victory that night.

Still, I have the consolation of having scored a few goals in the First Division. One other sticks out in my mind. I hit a 30-yarder over the 'keeper's head against Charlton. A good goal in any game, but even more so in a local derby!

The boss, John Docherty, picked it out as our 'goal of the season' for the Saint and Greavsie competition but my strike against Arsenal was even better.

But to be honest, I've got few complaints about my first year in the top flight. After playing so long in the Third and Fourth Divisions it was just great to visit all the big venues. Old Trafford, Anfield, White Hart Lane make a bit of a chance from Aldershot, Darlington and places like that!

I'm proud of everything we have achieved at the club in the last few years, on and off the field. Winning the Division Two title, and holding our own in the First, was

tremendous. But just as satisfying was the progress we have made off the field.

Millwall is a club of the people. It was great for us to win a prestigious award for our community programme last season. It showed we were getting things right as a club.

It was disappointing for me that a groin injury forced me to drop out of a couple of matches last season. One of them was the fixture against Newcastle United at St James' Park. That's one of the few Football League grounds I have yet to play on. With United being relegated, I won't have the chance to play there this season unless it's in a cup competition.

My old Wimbledon teammate Dave Beasant claims to have played on every League ground, and I can't be far short. I've certainly been up and down all the divisions.

JOHN DOCHERTY

I began my career at Chelsea, when they were a First Division side. But I never made the first team. I made my League debut for Hereford, and was in the side relegated from the Second Division in my first season.

I moved on to Wimbledon and helped them win promotion from the Fourth Division, before going back into the Fourth with Aldershot. But in the last five years, I've gone from the Third to the First with Millwall.

It means a lot to be successful with the Lions, because they're my local side. I was born at Lambeth. I feel at home with Millwall. I'd like to finish my playing career at the Den — but not for a while yet.

I'm 32 now, but every time someone mentions my age, I refer them to Billy Bonds. I'm just a youngster compared to Billy, who was playing First Division football for West Ham at the age of 41!

Bill has been an inspiration to people like Terry Hurlock and myself. He showed that, with the right attitude to training and playing, age is unimportant. I'm not worried about being able to last the pace in the First Division. I've no problems with my stamina or fitness. I believe I can carry on for a few years yet — though not perhaps as long as Billy Bonds!

Even though we slipped a little towards the end of last season, at one stage we were on the edge of the Championship race with less than a quarter of the season left.

Halfway through the season we had more wins, points and goals, than Liverpool (and Everton, Spurs and Manchester United). It just shows you don't have to be a so-called glamour club to survive at top level.

Millwall is a very homely club. It's tea and toast at the Den rather than caviar and champagne. We don't have any airs or graces. We just work hard and stay within our limitations.

It was great to see Terry Hurlock selected for the England 'B' tour last summer. It was a success he thoroughly deserved.

Like me, Terry had to wait a long time to play in the First Division. It shows the depth in our League that Terry was able to step up from Second Division football to the international scene, and more than hold his own.

I'm sure there are other players who have spent their lives in the lower divisions, who could bridge the gap, given the opportunity.

Success comes all the sweeter when you have to wait and work so long for it.

LEE CHAPMAN kicked off the current League season hoping that in the months to follow, he would be able to avoid last term's roller coaster.

The Nottingham Forest striker won't mind repeating some of the high spots which marked that campaign. But he can do without the low points which made it a season of mixed fortunes.

It began when the 29-year-old marksman was stranded in France, and, thanks to a legal wrangle, unable to kick a ball in competition.

Rescued by Forest, he hit the goal trail as the Midlands club went cup collecting. His five Littlewoods Cup strikes helped Forest reach Wembley, where they beat Luton Town 3-1 to lift the trophy.

That joy was forgotten just six days later as Chapman and his team-mates experienced the horror of the Hillsborough disaster during their FA Cup semi-final with Liverpool.

A return to Wembley in late April ended with Chapman scoring twice as Brian Clough's men beat Everton 4-3 in the Simod Cup Final.

Now Chapman is hoping for a season in which all the milestones are successful ones as he cements his place in a Forest side tipped to be a major challenger for honours once again.

But he acknowledges the fact that, if he'd had his way, he wouldn't even be playing League football in England now, far less lining up every week for Forest.

In the summer of last year, Lee decided to quit his previous English club, Sheffield Wednesday, and try life on the Continent with French side, Niort. It was to be the beginning of an exciting new chapter in his life — or so he anticipated. But within a few weeks it had all turned sour.

Says Lee, "In one respect, the move to French football was a way of providing myself with a new challenge in my career. But that was only part of the reason for going.

"I also wanted to sample a different way of life. I felt that I should widen my horizons, not wanting to spend the rest of my time knowing only one way of life — the English way.

"Playing football on the Continent was to be just a part of that new life. I realise it was a gamble and in the end I was unlucky that it didn't work out for me. But you can't go through life without taking risks.

"In the end I came home feeling quite philosophical about the whole affair. I certainly don't regret giving it a go, and it hasn't put me off doing it again sometime in the future.

"I simply chose the wrong club when I crossed the Channel last year. But my reasons for wanting to live on the Continent have not changed."

It all went wrong for Lee Chapman when Niort ran into serious financial problems just a few weeks after his arrival in France.

They were unable to raise the money to pay Sheffield Wednesday the transfer fee — and that left Lee in a Catch-22 situation.

Because they hadn't paid for him, Niort were told by UEFA that not only could they no longer play him in their French League fixtures, but it was also declared that he wasn't theirs to sell either! So until Sheffield Wednesday received their money, Chapman couldn't even be transferred to another outfit.

That made the whole thing infuriating for the player, because Forest, Derby County, Celtic, Chelsea, Queen's Park Rangers, Newcastle United — and even Sheffield Wednesday! — were interested in signing him.

Says Lee, "For me, the worst part of the whole affair was not knowing how it was all going to be resolved.

"It didn't help that there was a language problem which prevented me from fully grasping each development as it arose.

"To be honest, I don't think Niort handled the situation very well. In the end, they had to borrow money to pay Wednesday, then sell me in order to pay off the loan!"

For Chapman, the saving factor was that he was not alone during the ordeal. His wife, actress Leslie Ash — star of TV detective series "Cat's Eyes" — helped him through the worrying period.

And he admits that he had the satisfaction of at least playing some French League football before red tape curtailed his new career.

He goes on, "I've heard how difficult it can be for players moving abroad when they are not married.

"Having suffered my own predicament, I know it would have been a nightmare had I been over there on my own. But it was a great comfort to be able to go home at night and talk everything through with Leslie.

"As far as the playing side was concerned, I was barred from the side for only about three weeks. Nevertheless, it was a relief when everything was cleared up — and gratifying, too, to know that a number of British clubs were willing to welcome me back."

The events which were to make last season such a switchback ride for Chapman were typical of a career which had already seen more than its share of peaks and troughs.

A young star with Stoke City, Chapman was bought by Arsenal for half a million pounds in the summer of 1982. He was hailed as a great goalscoring prospect.

That move also turned out to be a disaster, however. The young

BRIAN CLOUGH

That sums up the season for Nottingham Forest striker LEE CHAPMAN.

Chapman's Highbury career lasted only 16 months.

During that period, he fell out of favour with manager Terry Neill — playing just 23 League matches in which he scored only four times — and became the butt of the North London boo-boys.

His subsequent move to Sunderland was just as calamitous. He lasted only half a season at Roker Park, scoring four times in his 15 appearances.

He recalls, "I just didn't know where I stood with Sunderland. When Len Ashurst took over from Alan Durban as manager, my future was in doubt.

"The new boss had his own ideas on which players were best suited for the club, and it was clear I wasn't one of them. Yet I'll always be sorry I wasn't given a real chance to show the fans what I could do."

His transfer valuation decreasing all the time, Chapman was next signed by Wednesday for £100,000 — and suddenly his career enjoyed a dramatic turnaround.

He immediately became a hit at Hillsborough, scoring 18 goals to re-establish the club in Division One in a season which he describes as "The best I'd ever had."

Four seasons were spent with Wednesday. And Chapman says of his association with the Yorkshire club, "It was perfect for me. At last I'd found a club which suited my style of play. The service from defenders and midfield was excellent. They got the ball into the box early and that helped me.

"My all-round game improved, helped by Howard Wilkinson, then the Wednesday manager. He encouraged me to become more involved outside the box.

"I helped in the build-ups and tried to create chances for others. Overall, my spell at Wednesday represented a complete rebirth of my career."

Now, of course, Chapman has his sights set on winning further honours with Forest.

He goes on, "I chose them ahead of all the others last season because manager Brian Clough had proved that he was capable of building an honours-winning side.

fortunes!

"I settled in well last term, but hopefully the Forest fans will now feel that they are seeing even better performances by me.

"Last season, even though I was pleased with my contribution, I was still getting to know everybody at the club. Not that it was a difficult task. In fact, the Forest side was such an easy one to slip into.

"Everything about the club is well-organised and well-disciplined. The pattern of the team was such that I didn't have too much trouble fitting in.

"Having said that, I knew I needed a period of readjustment following the very difficult three months I'd experienced in France.

"So I aimed to play my way in gradually and be at my peak this season. Hopefully, I'll continue to improve. When I arrived in Nottingham, I signed a four-year contract, and intend to remain loyal to the club during that period.

"I also intend to add further medals to my collection. I'm convinced that Forest are in the middle of an upswing in the club's fortunes. I mean to be around when the peak of that curve is reached," he closes.

CHRIS WADDLE *Spurs*

DARRON McDONOUGH (Luton Town) comes out on top in a high-stepping duel with Manchester United's **BRYAN ROBSON.**

RESCUED BY

GARY STEVENS ON THE TRANSFER THAT GAVE

WHEN I decided to join Rangers, I believed I'd be going to the biggest football club in Britain.

From what I'd been told about the set-up at Ibrox, and the ambitious plans they had for the future, I was also convinced I was about to become part of one of the biggest outfits in Europe, too.

In fact, if I had one doubt in my mind last summer, it was whether any club in Britain could be worthy of the

kind of build-up everyone was giving Rangers.

Yes, they were a huge club. But surely some of the things people said about them had to be exaggerated? I had the distinct impression that perhaps some people were painting a rosier picture than was true to life.

Now that I've spent a season at Ibrox, I can say in all honesty, that some of those folk WERE wrong.

RANGERS!
HIS CAREER A NEW LEASE OF LIFE.

Glasgow Rangers are a much BIGGER club than I was led to believe!

If I ever needed proof of that, it came in March when plans were unveiled to transform Ibrox Stadium into undoubtedly the best football ground in Britain.

An incredible £14 million is to be spent on increasing the stadium capacity to 52,000, as well as providing executive boxes — and even a stage for pop concerts. And yet, despite the big-spending, glamorous image that Rangers certainly have, I've never known a friendlier, family-type atmosphere at any other club.

Take last season's Skol Cup Final, for example. We had just beaten Aberdeen 3-2 in a magnificent match and I was delighted to have won my first medal in Scotland.

I'd planned to go out for a quiet meal later that night. Little did I know what was still in store for me.

From Hampden, the team bus headed straight back to Ibrox Park. When we made our entry up the famous marble staircase, I discovered that a couple of the club's huge hospitality suites had been turned over to the players and staff for a big celebratory party.

Instead of heading into town in small groups, as we would have done with my previous side Everton, the club made sure that we all had an unforgettable night at Ibrox. And that included everyone, from Graeme Souness right down to the kitchen staff and laundry ladies.

It's those little touches which make all the difference to a club. Even our kids aren't forgotten. On match days, Rangers provide a creche where our youngsters can play together and have a bit of a party on their own while the mums are in the stand watching "daddy" play.

As you can probably tell, I've never regretted my move north, despite the successful years I'd enjoyed at Everton.

I've regained my enthusiasm for the game which I was in danger of losing towards the end of my spell at Goodison Park. I needed new challenges, and moving to Rangers certainly provided them.

My last season with Everton was very disappointing. I felt I'd lost a lot of my form, and even four or five months into the season I found I was asking myself how I was going to regain it. Towards the end of that campaign, it became very hard to get motivated for games.

We had nothing left to play for and there was little hope that English clubs would be re-admitted to Europe. It was all very depressing.

Things really came to a head, however, following England's disastrous showing in the European Championships in West Germany. I just felt so flat when I came back that I knew a move would be the only way to revitalise my career. Looking back, I know I made the right decision — for all concerned.

I'd been at Everton since I was an apprentice. I was in danger of becoming part of the furniture at Goodison Park. The club and I were beginning to take each other for granted. And that was doing no-one any good.

From what I'd read, I knew that Rangers were interested in me. And I think that made it easier when the time came to ask for a move.

Fortunately, Everton were very good about it. At first, they didn't want to let me go. But the worst thing they could have done would have been to say, 'You've signed a two-year contract, you'll have to honour it'.

I think they realised this, too. After a couple of weeks of waiting, I went on holiday, and came back to find they'd agreed to my request. Fortunately, Graeme Souness came in for me immediately.

I wouldn't have left Everton for any club other than Rangers. I don't even know if any English sides had shown an interest in me — but it wouldn't have mattered if they had.

I wanted to move to a big club, and there simply aren't any bigger anywhere in Europe than Rangers.

Believe it or not, stamps and a saxophone have helped me become a better player for Glasgow Rangers.

How come?

Well, when I first arrived in Glasgow, Rangers put me up in a city hotel, then

a club flat, until my new home was built.

As any footballer in a similar situation will testify, living in a hotel for any length of time, no matter how plush, is a far cry from an ideal situation. You just can't avoid getting bored when you're separated from your family and friends.

I must admit I think I'd have been driven up the wall after my four months in the hotel if I hadn't had my stamp collection with me to keep me occupied.

Most footballers enjoy the usual types of hobbies when they're away from the game, such as playing snooker, golf, or watching videos. But I prefer philately. I must admit it's a fairly unusual hobby for a football player. I don't know of any others who share this pastime.

It's been a family interest for some time now. My dad was a keen collector and handed his album on to me when I was about 14. I've built up a fair collection since then, but it was when I first came to Glasgow that the album really came into its own.

I had a lot of spare time, especially in the afternoons, so I'd take out the telephone directory and hunt for the stamp shops in the city. Then I could rummage around to my heart's content, looking for any useful additions to my collection. I suppose part of the interest is the fact that you might just pick up a rare stamp, or a collector's item.

Once, in a dealer's shop in Liverpool, I came across a stamp which had a slight flaw. It was in an envelope full of ordinary stamps, and when I asked the dealer how much he wanted for it, he sold it to me for just 50 pence.

When I checked my reference books back home, I was surprised and delighted to discover that, because of the flaw, the stamp was worth something in the region of £400!

I suppose that's the real interest, using the knowledge you've gained to discover something that other people might overlook.

The other great hobby I have is one that's a bit less sedate. I'm learning to play the saxophone!

It's something I'd fancied trying since I was a youngster, but I'd never got round to it. I soon put that right when I moved into my club flat.

It's funny how these things get off the ground. I doubt if I'd ever have taken it up if I hadn't mentioned my interest to a taxi driver who regularly picked me up at my hotel.

He said he knew someone who'd played sax on a few albums, and put me in touch with him.

I'm not all that good yet as I haven't been practising all that long. If I stick in I might be worth listening to in a few years.

Of course, the big problem with the saxophone is that there's simply no way you can play it quietly. So practice isn't always easy — especially with my two-year-old son, Adam, around.

He usually likes to take a nap in the afternoons, and though I've tried stuffing a few of his cuddly toys down the bell of the instrument to muffle the sound, it doesn't really work!

Thankfully though, I haven't fallen out with any of my neighbours over the noise!

DAVID KELLY *West Ham*

ON THE AIR!

How Middlesbrough's ALAN KERNAGHAN is making his name off-the-field.

ON CUE — Alan Kernaghan (left) with Mark Page.

Middlesbrough striker Alan Kernaghan regularly finds himself in a spin. But it has nothing at all to do with football! Big Al is a budding radio D.J. . . . thanks to a friendship struck up with former Radio One presenter and Boro' fanatic Mark Page.

Mark now has regular slots on Radio Cleveland, Radio Clyde, Radio Luxembourg and B.F.B.S., the Forces network. Alongside him during all bar the Radio Clyde broadcast is Alan.

"I've always been into music," explains Al. "But it was only after I met up with Mark that I got the chance to go on the air myself.

"It began when I asked if I could pop into the Radio Cleveland studios to see how things operated. From that first visit Mark asked if I'd fancy doing a brief spot reviewing four or five new releases every Saturday morning.

"I jumped at the chance and it has taken off from there. Since then Mark's given me the opportunity to also work with him on Radio Luxembourg and B.F.B.S. It's been marvellous experience.

"As well as working the turntables, I've also done interviews with my Boro' team-mates on football and now there is a chance I'll be joining Mark on a Forces Television Network show!"

Fergie's Fledglings . . . Fergie's Babes . . . the Rookie Reds . . . That's how Manchester United's influx of young talent was toasted last season.

Manager Alex Ferguson shook the cobwebs off a youth policy at Old Trafford that had been badly neglected ever since Sir Matt Busby retired as boss.

The Scot thrust his promising kids into the full glare of the first-team spotlight. A bold act which wasn't all down to an injury crisis.

Ferguson's decision to put his faith in a batch of lads barely out of their teens — and some even who weren't — proved to be the move that rescued United's campaign from being a complete flop.

For two months in mid-season, the raw skill and enthusiasm of youth pepped up United's old hands and the crowds flocked back to Old Trafford.

Whilst the initial impact petered out as tired legs and injuries took their toll, the youngsters proved once again that Manchester United were back as leading lights in the talent-grooming stakes.

The lad who led the way and proved to be the cream of the crop was the youngest of the lot, **LEE SHARPE.**

His 17th birthday had been celebrated only a month previously when Alex Ferguson snapped him up from Fourth Division Torquay United. A down payment of £50,000 rose to £180,000 as cheques were sent regularly south as Lee passed certain landmarks.

One such extra payment was paid when Sharpe, after only six months at Old Trafford, was called up to the England Under-21 squad. He became the youngest-ever England international at that level when he was capped against Greece.

It put him alongside United's illustrious greats Duncan Edwards and George Best in the record books. They, too, were 17-year-olds when they first stepped on to an international stage.

Sharpe achieved all this after switching roles only weeks into his United career.

He was signed on the strength of his wing play for Torquay. However, he made his most telling contributions for United when converted to a very capable left-back.

Despite his tender years, Lee is already a sturdy six-footer with a powerful frame that hasn't finished filling out yet! Couple that with his pace, all-round ability and versatility and Ferguson has some player on his hands.

No wonder the United manager has predicted that Sharpe is a surefire certainty to win a full England cap in the future.

RUSSELL BEARDSMORE — Has the looks and hairstyle of the one-time Eastenders' character 'Lofty'. And despite attempts to put on weight the 20-year-old still tips the scales at a little over nine stone even when dripping wet!

Yet this unlikely lad proved that with Ferguson's sensible guidance last term he could withstand the rigours of the First Division.

None of the babes quite captured the hearts of the Old Trafford followers like little Beardsmore did. The roar that went up whenever he was introduced to the action from the substitutes' bench was one reserved for heroes!

A phenomenon Ferguson puts down to the fact that Russell in some ways reminds him of former Stretford End favourite Nobby Stiles.

It was the success of Beardsmore that the United boss admits forced him to bring forward the whole youth programme at Old Trafford and give more of the up-and-coming brigade a run in the senior side.

LEE MARTIN — Earned an England Under-21 call-up at the same time as Sharp and Beardsmore and his manager believes the local-born defender could eventually take up a berth at full cap level.

When he was promoted on a regular basis to the first team he was already the perfect build for a

FERGIE'S NEW FACES

How Manchester United's youngsters are grabbing their chance of stardom.

footballer. Tall and solid and with equal ability in both feet.

Whilst he was played mainly at right-back during his debut season, Martin was comfortable wherever he was played in the back four.

Sharpe, Beardsmore and Martin were the ones who could really claim they made the breakthrough last term but, backing them up with bit parts were Tony Gill, Deiniol Graham, Mark Robins and David Wilson.

In fact, when United began their FA Cup campaign against Queen's Park Rangers in January, all but the injured Sharpe took an active part in the match!

TONY GILL — Opened his senior goal-scoring account in the replay of that cup match and his strike was amongst the runners for Goal of the Season award. The Bradford-born 20-year-old's season sadly ended when he broke his leg in March.

RUSSELL BEARDSMORE

GIULIANO MAIORANA

LEE MARTIN

DEINIOL GRAHAM — A former star weight-lifter in his schooldays, the teenager made only a couple of substitute appearances but still managed to pop in a vital FA Cup goal in that time! A broken arm put paid to his progress.

MARK ROBINS — Mark Hughes and Brian McClair inevitably blocked the path of this goalscoring 19-year-old last term. Ferguson, however, rates him so highly that he's sure that if he'd been at any other club he would have been leading the attack.

Nevertheless the Oldham-born striker had a record for the reserves that kept Messrs Hughes and McClair on their toes.

He was by far the club's most prolific scorer at any level last year.

Mark was one of the first intake of boys chosen for the FA's National School of Excellence at Lilleshall in 1985.

DAVID WILSON — A midfielder from Burnley who was also a teenager when Ferguson pitched him into senior action.

GIULIANO MAIORANA — He wasn't given run-outs at the height of United's season because he was still working in a men's outfitters whilst playing his football for non-League Histon in the Jewson East Anglia League!

Maiorana's skills were raw but Alex Ferguson and his team of talent-spotters saw enough in the tricky winger to pay £30,000.

TV viewers also saw enough in a televised League game against

Arsenal last term, when 'Jules' went on a couple of mazy runs, to realise that, once United have smoothed off his rough edges, the teenager with an Italian family could be exciting the Old Trafford crowd for years to come.

When Alex Ferguson first arrived at United, he was puzzled and embarrassed by the way neighbours Manchester City were cornering the market in young talent.

Now he's licked the youth policy into shape and given a chance to youngsters, the talk at the famous club is of the comparison with the talented young boys who came through under Sir Matt Busby's guidance.

Ferguson sensibly played down such talk and has nurtured his kids along without asking too much too early and ruining them.

The arrival of so many youngsters has brought a welcome breath of fresh air to Manchester United. No longer is the cheque book the only answer to their problems.

TERRY HURLOCK *Millwall*

It'll be the greatest ever!

That's the boast of Italy as they prepare to stage the 1990 World Cup Finals.

Every four years the claim is made. The next World Cup Finals will be the richest, biggest, most spectacular yet staged. Quite often the claim is justified, but some years the organisation doesn't match the hype.

But when the football-mad Italians set out to make the 1990 competition the greatest so far, they put their money where their mouth is — £200,000,000 of it!

That's how much the Italian government set aside to make the twelve World Cup grounds the most modern and well-equipped ever to stage the Finals.

In Italian money it amounts to a staggering 460 BILLION lire. For that cash the Italians will get two completely new top-class stadiums — at Turin and Bari — and ten established grounds re-built and modernised.

Around £24 million will be spent on the already magnificent Olimpico Stadium in Rome, where the World Cup Final will be staged on July 8. The stadium has already hosted an Olympic Games, and a European Championships final. But the Italians decided it wasn't up to scratch for their super-duper World Cup.

In June the Olympic Stadium closed for a year. It means Roma and Lazio, the two Italian First Division giants who share the ground, moving to an alternative stadium for a season. Their own ground is being ripped apart and almost completely rebuilt to provide 85,000 seats under cover.

More than £20 million will be spent on a brand new 58,000 seater stadium at Bari. About £19 million on a 70,000 all-seat ground in Turin.

The Friuli stadium at Udine was built only 14 years ago. It gets the smallest amount of money for modernisation — only £8 million!

The Italians aim to recoup all this cash from the increased tourism, and from sponsors. Eight Italian companies were appointed as 'Official Suppliers' to the World Cup — at a cost to each one of over £3 million. They include names like car-makers Fiat, airline Alitalia, typewriter giant Olivetti, and the Italian State Railways.

Another supplier is the Banco Nationale del Lavoro. For their £3 million they get the privilege of being the official ticket agency for the World Cup. All ticket sales in Italy will be through the bank.

A total of 2,600,000 tickets went on sale for the World Cup Finals — an average of 50,000 for each of the 52 matches in the competition. In the first month of sales, 365,000 tickets were sold in Italy alone.

Cheapest tickets for first round matches cost around £7.00, with the most expensive seats at over £40.00. Cheapest tickets for the final will be around £12.00, and the best seats in the Olympic Stadium will cost not far short of £100.00.

The format of the World Cup Finals in Italy will be the same as in Mexico four years ago. 24 finalists split into six groups of four. The top two from each group qualifying for the knock-out stages along with the four best 'third-placed' teams.

One hundred and three countries finally took part in the qualifying rounds, playing a total of 336 group matches. Those nations were playing for 22 places in Italy, with the hosts, and the holders, Argentina, joining them.

The big kick-off in Italy is timed for 6 p.m. at the Giuseppe Meazza stadium in Milan, on June 8. The stadium has been rebuilt at a cost of £21 million, with a horse-shoe shaped third 'tier' constructed over the original stands.

Two thousand, two hundred and eighteen newspaper reporters, 300 photographers, and 513 radio and T.V. commentators will be there.

Each press seat will be equipped with an 11-inch monitor screen with six channels, including one for the game being played, a televideo channel, and a closed circuit channel linked to the interview and press conference room.

Press interviews will be accompanied by simultaneous translation into five different languages.

Italian Radio and Television are constructing a new International Broadcasting Centre on a 20,000 square metre site in Rome, to be the technical 'brain' of the T.V. and radio operation.

They expect a new world record television audience to watch the transmission of the World Cup final. In 1986 an estimated 652 million viewers worldwide, in 166 countries, watched Argentina beat West Germany in Mexico. The Italians expect 1.6 billion viewers.

Italian plans are all going smoothly. It's looking like the greatest World Cup of all. But taking a keen interest in all the pre-World Cup build-up are the Americans. They have been awarded the World Cup Finals for 1994.

And you know the Americans. Anything you can do, they can do bigger. Their World Cup will be THE BEST. (Until 1998!)

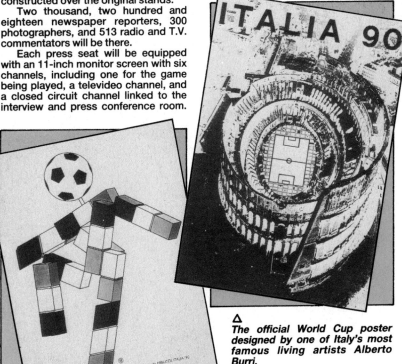

△
The official World Cup poster designed by one of Italy's most famous living artists Alberto Burri.

◁ *The World Cup mascot.*

I'LL ALWAYS BE A WEDNESDAY FAN!

Says Sheffield Wednesday's CHRIS TURNER.

TO say I breathed a sigh of relief when we beat Middlesbrough 1-0 on the final Saturday of last season's League programme is a major understatement! That victory meant we kept our place in the First Division, which for a club like Sheffield Wednesday was absolutely crucial.

I knew that better than most people. I was a Wednesday fan as a youngster. It's my home town club and I'm now in my second spell at Hillsborough.

As a youngster of eleven, I stood on the terraces and watched Wednesday lose their final home match to Manchester City and slide into Division Two. I well recall how upset I was, so I knew exactly how our fans felt nearly twenty years on.

Not only that, after slipping into the Second, Wednesday ended up in the Third, which is where they were when I signed on as a professional in the mid-70's. I knew that if we had gone down last season it could have set the club back five years.

Relegation would have certainly undone all the good work done by the man who signed me for this second stint at the club, Howard Wilkinson. He and Peter Eustace, his assistant, had dragged the Owls up to the First from the Third. It would have been a tragedy if that progress had been wasted.

Howard signed me from Manchester United at the start of last season but left to take over as boss of Leeds three weeks later.

I must confess I felt let down by that. No disrespect to Howard, but that's the last thing a new signing needs.

A manager buys you because he rates you. He puts his money down on the table to back up his judgment. But when he leaves, you are passed on to someone who might not hold the same opinion.

I was fortunate. Howard's successor was his assistant, Peter Eustace, with whom I'd worked in the past, so I didn't suffer as some players do.

But by then we were beginning to struggle. Our start hadn't been too bad. We'd been defending well though not scoring too many goals. But we had an awful spell at Christmas, losing 3-0 at home to Nottingham Forest and 5-0 at Coventry.

RON ATKINSON

It was uphill all the way after that until Ron Atkinson took over from Peter Eustace in February. I knew Ron from my days at Old Trafford. In fact, he had signed me from Sunderland in 1985. I knew when I heard his name being put forward as a possible Wednesday boss that he was the man for the job.

Ron has a big personality but he has never let that get in the way of the work he puts in on the training pitch and from his office. He is very definitely not just a figurehead.

I knew from working with him at United that he would lift the players and restore confidence which had been dented badly by our poor results. That's exactly what happened.

Ron likes his teams to play bright attacking football. Above all he wants to entertain. Even knowing that playing that way we might concede a few more goals than with a dour defensive formation, I'd much prefer to play in an attacking team.

Ron also bought three new players — Carlton Palmer, Dave Bennett and Steve Whitton — who all did great jobs for us during the run-in.

As the season closed it looked as if we might face a battle to keep Ron as boss. He had taken over on only a temporary basis and there were rumours that he might be tempted back to Spain, where he had had a spell with Athletico Madrid earlier last season.

It would have been disastrous to lose him. He is one of the best, if not THE best, manager we could possibly have had. Plus, having had three managers in the space of

eight months, his departure would have done nothing for the continuity of the club. The three lads he had bought would have felt let-down as I did when Howard Wilkinson went to Leeds.

Fortunately Ron agreed to sign a new contract and we as players, as well as the fans, could look forward this term to building on last season's survival.

I still class myself very much as a fan. When I pack in the game, Wednesday will be the club I come to watch. Even while I was with Sunderland and Manchester, I tracked the club's fortunes.

I don't regret the nine years I spent away from Hillsborough. I enjoyed the experience at both clubs, even though I always had the hope that one day I'd return.

When I left, Wednesday were in the Third Division. I was out of contract and the manager at the time, Jack Charlton, was not playing me in the team.

Sunderland and Watford came in for me and I chose Roker Park because the manager, Ken Knighton, had been a coach at Hillsborough during my early days at the club.

Nine years is a long time to be away from a club and when I returned last season my reaction was mixed.

I had a clear feeling of coming home. Yet everything had changed so much it was almost like joining a new club.

When I returned there wasn't a single player or member of the coaching staff who was at the club when I left. I'm sure, too, that many of the people who support Wednesday these days didn't come to the ground when I was here the first time.

I came back as an experienced professional who was expected to show a good example to the younger lads.

I feel that's the responsibility of every senior pro, though, unfortunately, there are those who don't do it. Young lads take their lead from the older players and if the senior man is not putting in the effort in training and his attitude isn't spot on, it rubs off.

I've always tried to do things right and last season I reckoned I put in more work than I've ever done. I hope it paid off during the relegation fight. And I hope it will help me be part of a successful Sheffield Wednesday in the coming years.

H

DAVE BEASANT
Chelsea

ROB JOHNSON
Luton

I MAY be coming to the end of my twelfth year with Celtic, but I can honestly say I'm as happy at Parkhead today as I was when I first arrived.

I've always supported the club because of family ties. My great uncle Willie was both a player and manager there. So when Celtic came in for me it was an easy decision to put pen to paper to join the team I love.

I'd been down for trials with Leeds, while Nottingham Forest and Chelsea had also expressed an interest in me, but it was no contest as soon as Celtic came on the scene.

In these days when people criticise players for not being loyal to their clubs, I suppose I'm one of the few exceptions. But I believe a major reason for remaining with one team is happiness.

If you enjoy doing something, that's the most important thing. It doesn't matter what it is, whether it be acting, painting or whatever. If you get pleasure from what you are doing, it makes it all worthwhile.

Eight years after making my first-team debut, I still get a buzz from pulling on the green-and-white jersey for Celtic. That feeling will probably never leave me, which is why a move to Europe or England has not appealed to me.

I can still remember clearly the events that led up to me getting my first-team chance at the age of seventeen. Charlie Nicholas, Mike Conroy and Dom Sullivan were all injured, and I was told I'd be playing.

I found it hard to grasp at first that I was about to make my debut for the team I loved.

My first three years in the side proved to be my learning period. I know I've still a lot to improve on even now, but that part of my career was very important to me.

It's only in the last few years that I've finally shaken off the 'wonder-boy' tag which had hung around my shoulders since my early days in the side. I'm pleased it's been lifted at last. But even when I was younger I never really found it too much of a burden.

All players, even if they come into a side at an early age, are expected to produce the goods consistently. I look at lads like John Collins of Hibs and fully understand just how much pressure he's under every week as a result of these demands. And I was just as aware that many people expected great things from me because I was a

WHY CELTIC SUIT ME!

PAUL McSTAY gives his reasons for being happy at Parkhead.

youngster when I broke into the team.

Maybe it has something to do with eventually losing my 'great potential' tag, but certainly in the last two seasons I believe I've played some of the best football of my career. This was underlined in the 1987-89 season when Celtic won the double and I was voted Player of the Year by my fellow professionals and by the Scottish Football Writers' Association.

Last season's League campaign was an uphill battle for us compared to the previous campaign, but we did manage to lift the Scottish Cup, beating our arch-rivals Rangers in the Final. That gave me a great deal of satisfaction.

So has being involved with Scotland's international plans in recent years.

I'd been part of the Scottish side which won the 1982 World Youth Cup under Andy Roxburgh. That helped me when he took charge of the national squad. He knew exactly what I had to offer, and I knew all about him.

He was the man who predicted early in my career that I would win 100 caps, which, at the time, I have to admit, was something I just laughed off.

It certainly never crossed my mind when I made my Scotland debut in 1984 in a friendly at Hampden against Uruguay. But with nearly 40 at the moment, I believe it's not an unrealistic target to aim for.

I love the challenge international football presents. Facing foreign players is a great way of finding out how good you are.

But, to be honest, I really am just happy being involved with the set-up. I've only missed one game since Andy took over and I like to think I could continue that run. I reckon that, at most, I've another ten years at the top.

And with the number of international games we now play every season, my hope is I can achieve the same milestone as my boyhood

ANDY ROXBURGH

hero, Kenny Dalglish, and become Scotland's most-capped player.

However, you never know when your international career might end. Injury or loss of form could finish it just as quickly as it began. My main aim is simply to enjoy it while I can.

When Mr Roxburgh took over as national coach in 1986, some of the older players weren't sure quite what to expect. Now, though, they know just how good a coach he is.

Many of the younger ones, like myself, didn't need to be convinced. We'd experience of him and his assistant Craig Brown at Youth level and knew they'd be a success in the job.

That's gone a long way to making this the happiest international squad I've ever been involved with. You look forward to meeting up for matches because there is such a good atmosphere.

I think the fact we all work hard for each other stems in many ways from the spirit which exists in the camp. Our 2-0 victory over France in the World Cup Qualifying match at Hampden in March was typical of the way we now work as a team to achieve good results.

That's why I'm always surprised to hear fans say after a bad Scotland display that there doesn't seem to be any pride in playing for our country anymore. Nothing could be further from the truth. There's always something special about wearing a Scotland shirt.

I'm just like any fan who dreams of representing his country. The only difference is that I've been given the chance. The other players all feel the same way.

I realise the people who expect me to do well at club level are also looking for the same level of performance from me in the internationals.

But, in a role that requires me to be the play-maker, I'm under no illusions about what is required of me. I need to help make the team tick. So if I'm setting up goals for others, I feel I'm doing what

I'm there for.

Not that I don't enjoy having the odd crack at goal myself. Goal-scoring is one area of my game I would like to improve. I feel I need to get on the score-sheet more often. During my League career, my highest total in a season has been eight, so I'm looking for double figures — at least — this time round.

The pressure it takes off the main strikers when a midfielder weighs in with a few is so important. Unfortunately, I don't seem to be too lucky in front of goal these days. Last season, three of my strikes were ruled out for infringements by team-mates, which just proves my point.

But this area of my game is not the only one I'd like to improve. Every aspect of my play could be better. I'd like to think our fans have yet to see the best of me.

One thing I am happy with is the fact I'm playing my football in Scotland. The game up here has been on a real high for some time, and there are a number of good young players coming through, so the future of the game looks bright.

In midfield alone, a few new stars have already caught my eye. John Collins has impressed me. Rangers' midfield trio of Ian Durrant, Derek and Ian Ferguson have proved, too, that they can cope with the demands of the Premier League.

Outwith the Scottish game, there are a couple of stars I rate highly. Glenn Hoddle has been a tremendous player for years, first at Tottenham and now with Monaco. He has the ability to inspire players around him.

The other may not be so well known, but I believe he's just as good — Michel of Real Madrid. I've come up against him when we've played Spain. And on every occasion he's turned on the style. What a dream it would be to play alongside both of them every week.

But, as I said at the start, I'm happy to be part of the Celtic team.

GARY PALLISTER
Middlesbrough

DENNIS WISE
Wimbledon

it's a girls' game, TOO!

SO SAYS MICHELE COCKBURN, THE FOOTBALL ASSOCIATION'S FIRST FULLY-QUALIFIED FEMALE COACH

A MINI revolution is quietly getting off the ground in one of the male strongholds of football — the North-West.

The area that houses the giants of English soccer, Liverpool, Everton and Manchester United, has become the testing ground for the development of women's football.

Females and soccer has long been a partnership sneered at in many quarters. The young woman charged with the task of changing that attitude is Michele Cockburn.

The 27-year-old hails from Newcastle. But despite her roots being firmly planted in a hot bed of soccer, Michele's earlier sporting interests were guided down the usual road for girls.

Football was strictly for the boys. With no encouragement forthcoming to don a soccer kit or drape a Newcastle scarf around her neck, Michele took up netball and hockey, right and proper games for girls.

It is those kind of attitudes that the Geordie lady is intent on changing.

And for those who laugh at the idea of a woman in the football world then Michele has the perfect answer... a fully-qualified FA coach's badge!

A two-week residential course at the FA's coaching centre at Lilleshall in the summer of '87 saw her emerge from the lectures, theory papers and practical coaching work as the first female to achieve the full FA coaching badge!

"To be accepted you need to have as much clout behind you as possible," says Michele, "and that clout doesn't come bigger than an FA coaching badge. I can turn round to anyone who might snigger at me and say to them, 'I know what I'm talking about'."

And she certainly does. A fact recognised by the Women's

Football Association when, at the start of this year, they appointed Michele as the north-west's development officer.

Her task in that area is to sow the seeds at grass roots level in the hope that they will spread nationwide and change the outlook on women's football.

"I wasn't encouraged to take an interest in football at all at an early age," Michele points out. "That only developed at college when I was training to be a PE teacher. Young girls and boys in the schools where I worked were always separated for their sport classes. I thought, why not mix them?

"I was given the go-ahead to do just that and I organised the football lessons. The kids loved it and soccer really took off amongst the girls.

"So much so that because they were not allowed to play for the boys' school team, I ran a 5-a-side competition amongst local schools for the girls. That became extremely popular.

"We were encouraging them to play as early as seven years old. That's the level we have to start at if women's football is to make good progress."

Michele admits that progress will be slow initially. Breaking down the barriers which stand in the way of female soccer won't be done overnight.

She's concentrating at present on travelling the north-west urging schools to introduce soccer for girls and passing on her knowledge of setting up teams and leagues.

"Teachers come to me and say that they have a really talented girl footballer and it's a shame she's not allowed in the boys' team. My reply is that there are probably four more girls in the school interested in football. So why not form a 5-a-side team, then contact a local school and see if they could do likewise?" Michele explains.

"That's how these kind of leagues can grow and keenness for the sport amongst girls can develop with them."

Currently there are 36 women's teams affiliated to their amateur league and the national side is self-financed, unlike some of its continental counterparts.

Clearly a long hard slog is ahead for Michele Cockburn before her dream of a semi-professional Superleague comes about.

However, the tremendous hard work she's putting in at the grass roots level could see that dream turn to reality.

IAN MILLER *Blackburn Rovers*

DAVID SEAMAN
Queen's Park Rangers

STEVE MacKENZIE
Charlton

ON THE FUNNY SIDE!

ANSWERS
TO IT HAPPENED LAST SEASON ON P16

1. Mike Hooper.
2. Ipswich Town and Luton Town, respectively.
3. Glanford Park.
4. Theo Snelders of Aberdeen.
5. Charlton Athletic.
6. Manchester City's Nigel Gleghorn.
7. Stuart McCall in the FA Cup and Tony Cottee in the Simod Cup.
8. Morton.
9. Sergei Baltacha.
10. Rhys Wilmot.
11. Luther Blissett.
12. Mark Bright and Ian Wright.
13. David Oldfield.
14. Bolton Wanderers and Torquay United.
15. Ralph Milne.
16. Brian Mitchell.
17. Howard Wilkinson, Peter Eustace and Ron Atkinson.
18. Graham Roberts.
19. Sporting Gijon.
20. Colin Clarke.
21. Blackburn Rovers, Crystal Palace, Swindon Town and Watford.

YOUR PICTURE GUIDE
ACTION! PIN-UPS! COLOUR!

Printed and Published in Great Britain by D. C. THOMSON & CO., LTD., 185 Fleet Street, London EC4A 2HS.

© D. C. THOMSON & CO., LTD., 1989.

ISBN 0-85116-449-8

PICTURES TO BE PROUD OF!